Robert

THE
MAGNIFICENT
YANKEES

THE GRAND SLAM!—Rookie Gil McDougald hits home run with the bases filled against Larry Jansen of the Giants at the Polo Grounds in the fifth game of the 1951 World Series, third grand slam in Series history.

THE KID—There's a reason for Mickey Mantle's smile since he jumped in one season from a Class C shortstop to a Yankee outfielder.

THE MUSCLE MAN—Yogi Berra, iron-man catcher of the Yankees and the American League's Most Valuable Player for 1951.

THE SCOOTER—Phil Rizzuto, Yankee shortstop and one of the most dangerous bunters in baseball.

TOM MEANY

THE MAGNIFICENT YANKEES

The Big League Baseball Library

GROSSET & DUNLAP *Publishers*
NEW YORK

PREFACE

In starting a new series of sports books on major league baseball teams, A. S. Barnes & Co. deems it fitting and proper to inaugurate it with the New York Yankees, baseball's most successful team, which in 1952 celebrates its fiftieth year in the American League.

Rather than a chronological, statistical history of the Yankee franchise, this book is a series of profiles on its most recent stars, the players who were prominent in the winning of the American League pennants and World Championships in 1949, 1950 and 1951.

Most of the material in this book never appeared in print before and all that has been reprinted has been brought up to date. For permission to reprint, acknowledgment is gratefully made to A. S. Barnes & Co. for the chapters on Joe DiMaggio, Vic Raschi and Yogi Berra; to *Collier's* Magazine for the chapter on Mickey Mantle, to *Sport* Magazine for the chapters on Casey Stengel, Allie Reynolds and Jerry Coleman.

Acknowledgment also is made to the sports writers who assisted me in the preparation of material for this book— Milton Gross, Jerry Mitchell and Arch Murray of the New York *Post;* Ben Epstein of the New York *Daily Mirror* and Joe Trimble of the New York *Daily News.*

PREFACE

Thanks also is due for the fine cooperation of the Yankee publicity department, particularly to Miss Margaret Regetz, who assisted in the selection of photographs, and to J. G. Taylor Spink, publisher of *The Sporting News,* for permission to include in the appendix the individual records of the Yankees from *The Sporting News Register.*

Tom Meany

FOREWORD

After talking about the Yankees for so many years, it is a pleasure to read about them. And an added pleasure to write something about them. Tom Meany, who has been a close friend of mine ever since I first came to New York, has chosen an excellent title for this book, *The Magnificent Yankees*. For, believe me, folks, they have been magnificent through the years. It hasn't been just for one season, or for one World Series, but for over thirty years, ever since the late Miller Huggins piloted them to their first pennant in 1921.

Perhaps what has impressed me the most in my association with the Yankees has been what might be called "the chain of succession," the manner in which one star player has been succeeded by another. It has happened too often to be sloughed off as mere "Yankee luck." There is a pattern to it, a pattern which traces directly to the fine organizational work of the front office. Sometimes the replacement is a player who built a great reputation in the Yankee farm system, as Joe Gordon did before taking Tony Lazzeri's place, sometimes it is a comparative unknown as in the more recent cases of Jerry Coleman and Gil McDougald.

Broadcasting or telecasting ball games is not the soft snap

it may seem to the uninitiated. I'm not going to yammer that my job is killing me because I love my work but broadcasting a ball game means beating your gums to a vast audience for about three hours—sometimes longer. When you have to spout so many words into a microphone every day or night, it helps to have something to talk about—and the Yankees certainly have provided me with a great deal of conversation through the years.

The writers who have associated with Tom in putting this book together are well known to me and to the Yankee players, for they have traveled with the clubs and know the players they write about as well as they know the members of their own family. It gives *The Magnificent Yankees* a fine touch of authenticity.

Casey Stengel is the latest Yankee manager to publicly declare that there is something inspiring to a ball player in merely putting on a Yankee uniform. I believe that to be true. I know that my radio or television duties never brought me into contact with any athletic organization, in any sport, which had greater team spirit than the Yankees. And that goes for the Yankees of yesterday, the Yankees of today and, I am sure, the Yankees of tomorrow.

It must be more than an accident that no manager who ever managed the Yankees for longer than one full season failed to win a pennant with them in the last three decades.

How about that?

MEL ALLEN

New York, N.Y., February, 1952.

CONTENTS

CONTENTS

THE
MAGNIFICENT
YANKEES

CHAPTER I

"THE ORGANIZATION"

BY TOM MEANY

The greatest annual gathering of baseball figures is not, as you might suspect, the World Series in October but the minor league conventions in December. These meetings are, with few exceptions, held in a minor league city, while the major league meetings, which come a week later, are usually held in New York or in Chicago.

To these meetings come professional baseball people from all parts of the country. There are hundreds of job seekers crowding the lobby floors, many who were headline stars in their day, others who never got into the majors at all. The jobs they seek are as varied as the applicants—scouts, managers, umpires, front office men.

One of the features of this annual convention is a party thrown by the Yankees for their executives and scouts and for the New York press. Quite often, it is the only time the writers get a chance to see the scouts, who spend their summers combing the bushes, and it is the only time the business manager from Beaumont, Texas, gets a chance to insist that he needs a pitcher or the new manager of Binghamton, New York, has the opportunity to explain that he could use an outfielder who could hit the long ball.

These Yankee parties are pleasant and informal, with speeches remarkable for their brevity. Even Manager Casey Stengel manages to state his case in something under an hour. Stengel made his first speech under Yankee auspices in Minneapolis in 1948 at Hotel Radisson, in the course of which he made it plain that Yankee co-owners Dan Topping and Del Webb hadn't offered him the job because of friendship. He was expected to deliver, he said, and he added that he would do his best. When he spoke at the Athletic Club in Columbus at the Yankee dinner in December, 1951, he had won three pennants and three World's Championships with the Yankees.

"Right up here on the dais with me," declared Stengel, with a generous sweep of his arm to indicate the Yankee brass, "and right out here in front of me are the people who made it possible for me to win those pennants. They kept the players coming to me. All I had to do was use 'em. The organization won the pennants."

While Stengel was overly modest, perhaps, in giving all the credit to "the organization," there is no doubt that the pennants couldn't have been won without it. The Yankees, even though for 1953 they reduced their farm clubs to ten, are a mighty baseball empire. In their system they have clubs at Kansas City in the American Association (Class AAA), Birmingham in the Southern (AA), Binghamton in the Eastern (A), Norfolk in the Piedmont (B), Quincy in the Three-Eye (B), Joplin in the Western Association (C), Boise in the Pioneer (C), McAlester in the Sooner State (D), Olean in the Pony (D), and Owensboro in the Kitty (D).

4

At one time, the Yankees had as many as 22 minor league affiliates, but General Manager George Weiss, in being forced to trim down for a variety of reasons, including television and the military draft, has decided to concentrate on quality. The Yankee record would indicate that he has been getting it.

Weiss runs the Yankees. President Dan Topping is perfectly willing to let George do it, since he knows he couldn't get a better man. The Topping-Del Webb administration is the fourth under which Weiss has served the Yankees and served them well. He came to the organization in February, 1932, when the late Colonel Jacob Ruppert was the Yankee president. After the Colonel's death in January, 1939, George served under Ed Barrow, who had been Ruppert's general manager, and then under the tumultuous Larry MacPhail from 1945 through 1947. The night the Yankees won the World Series in '47, Larry highlighted the victory party at the Hotel Biltmore by firing Weiss. Within 24 hours, MacPhail had been bought out by his partners, Topping and Webb, and Weiss's contract had been upped from $35,000 to $50,000.

Weiss, who had operated ball clubs in New Haven and Baltimore before the Yankees brought him in in 1932 to lay the foundations for their farm system, has gained in stature with the years. Because he operated under the shadow of Barrow first and then MacPhail, there were some who expressed doubts about his ability to go it alone.

"George is a fine No. 2 man," said his critics, "but he hasn't enough class to be head man."

Four straight pennants and four World's Championships in the last four years of George's five-year reign as head man have silenced the critics.

Quiet and soft-spoken, Weiss sticks to his guns with great

tenacity, as ball players waging holdout battles have learned. As a trader, George is one of the best. He has been so shrewd in his baseball deals that it has more than once been suggested that George, rather than Joe DiMaggio, should be known as the Yankee Clipper.

Weiss's baseball career almost came to a tragic end when it was just starting. He was president of the New Haven Club in the Eastern League in 1923 and on his way to the minor league meetings with his manager, Wild Bill Donovan, who had been a famous pitcher with the Tigers and Dodgers and once a Yankee manager. George and Bill shared a drawing room.

"The only reason I'm alive today is that I don't smoke," relates Weiss. "When we were ready to turn in, Bill said he thought he'd go up to the club car and smoke a cigar before going to bed. Since I didn't smoke, I told him I'd hit the hay.

"Our berths were made up and I climbed into the upper, thinking that I might be asleep before Bill returned and it would be more convenient for him to take the lower.

"I was still awake when Donovan came back and he wanted to switch with me, saying it didn't look right for the president to be sleeping in an upper while the manager had a lower. I said it made no difference to me, that I was comfortable where I was. We said good-night and fell asleep."

During the night, there was a train crash. Donovan, in the lower berth, was killed instantly and Weiss was badly injured. Had George exercised the owner's perogative and taken the lower berth he would have been killed.

"Yankees" is the best known nickname in baseball, yet nobody knows who thought it up. Some historians, Grantland

Rice, dean of American sports writers among them, set the date as around 1908 when Yankees first supplanted "Highlanders" as the nickname for the American League Baseball Club of New York. That last mouthful, incidentally, was the corporate title of the club until MacPhail came along in 1945 and officially made the title "The Yankees, Inc."

The popular belief is that a harassed headline writer, fed up with trying to crowd the 11-letter Highlanders into a headline, devised instead the 7-letter Yankees, which had the additional advantage of permitting a curtailment to the 5-letter Yanks.

The Yankees have won the most pennants (19) and the most world championships (15) but things weren't always lush for them. Their beginnings were humble. In January, 1903, Ban Johnson, president of the infant American League, dug up two men, Frank Farrell, a race-horse owner and plunger, and Bill Devery, a former police commissioner, to back a team in New York in the new league. The Baltimore franchise, virtually wrecked six months before when John McGraw jumped it to come to the Giants and take his stars with him, was purchased by Farrell and Devery for $18,000 and moved to New York.

There was no spacious stadium for the Yanks to play in then. A ball park with a wooden grandstand was built up near where the Medical Center now stands. It was called Hilltop Park, which may explain how the new American League team came up with its nickname of Highlanders, a fancy derivative of Hilltoppers.

It was 1913 before the feud with the Giants simmered down sufficiently to permit the Yankees to share the Polo Grounds with them, under a policy of cooperation still fol-

7

lowed in St. Louis and Philadelphia, where the two leagues work out of one park. By 1915, Colonel Jacob Ruppert, the brewer, and Tillinghast L'Hommidieu Huston, took over the Yankees from Farrell and Devery.

Huston, a self-made man who was called "Cap" because of his service in Cuba in the Spanish-American war and later was to become a Colonel in World War I, didn't see eye-to-eye with Ruppert on many things, principally the selection of little Miller Huggins as Yankee manager instead of Cap's hunting and drinking companion, Wilbert Robinson.

Ruppert was aristocratic and autocratic. Huston was rough and ready. It was obvious the partnership couldn't continue very long. That it lasted until the spring of 1923, was due only to the fact that Huston was overseas during the war. By now the Yankees had acquired Babe Ruth and were outstripping the Giants as drawing cards. This was more than McGraw could stand and he moved them out of the Polo Grounds. It was one of the most costly spite fences ever built, for the Yanks moved across the Harlem and erected their own magnificent stadium.

Shortly after the Stadium opened in 1923—with a home run by Babe Ruth, of course—Huston sold out his 50 per cent to Ruppert for $1,500,000, a far cry from the $18,000 Devery and Farrell had put up to buy the club originally, or the $400,000 Ruppert and Huston had paid for the franchise in 1915.

The Yanks continued under the Ruppert banner, with Ed Barrow, who came on in October, 1920, as general manager, running the organization for Colonel Jake. Barrow ran the club for the estate after Ruppert's death in 1939 until 1945, when MacPhail engineered the deal which bought the franchise for himself, Topping and Webb for a reported $3,400,000. And Larry bowed out 32 months later with better than $1,000,000 for his one-third.

MacPhail did a great deal for the Yanks, although he parted company on such an acrimonious note that those he left behind don't care to sing his praises. He put in the lights, which prepared the way for the seasonal attendance of two million-plus, and he renovated a ball plant and a farm system that was rapidly succumbing to dry rot. He streamlined and modernized the entire minor league setup.

Weiss has carried on the work of the organization in the Yankee tradition. He has able assistants, such as Roy Hamey, former general manager at Kansas City, president of the American Association and right-hand man at Pittsburgh to Frank McKinney. Parke Carroll, general manager at Kansas City, and Lee MacPhail, co-relator of the minor league system, are other valued aides.

One of the most valuable members of the Yankee office staff is Arthur E. (Red) Patterson, whose official title is press and promotions director but whose energies are all encompassing. Red is priceless to the Yankees in keeping them before the public during the long winter months when news is at a minimum. Patterson, a former baseball writer and, strangely enough, dog editor, of the New York *Herald Tribune,* joined MacPhail in 1946, starting out as traveling secretary, a job now handled by Bill McCorry.

Despite executives like Barrow, MacPhail and Weiss and managers such as Huggins, Joe McCarthy, Bucky Harris and Stengel, the Yankees couldn't have won their 19 pennants without ball players. And they wouldn't have had the ball players without scouts. Paul Krichell, the discoverer of Lou Gehrig, is the best known of the Yankee scouts today, now that his two West Coast confreres, Joe Devine and Bill Essick, have passed on.

Scouts are the most underpublicized and least understood members of any baseball organization. A writer once referred to them as "the chorus men of baseball," since rarely does the average fan see or hear anything of them.

No longer is scouting a one-man job. Back before World War I, the Dodgers had what amounted to a one-man scouting staff in the late Larry Sutton. He dug up such stars as Zack Wheat, Nap Rucker, Jake Daubert, Casey Stengel, Dazzy Vance and Hank DeBerry for a total sum that today would look like one scout's expense account for a two-week trip.

Prospects are usually flushed by what the trade terms "bird dogs," men who work on a commission basis. They report each find to a regular scout, who takes a look-see and reports back to the home office. This starts the beginning of a file on the youth and other scouts are sent from time to time to keep checking. All reports are filed away and within a couple of months, the envelope on any young player is bulging.

Reports do not stop after the prospect has been signed. Scouts check and re-check and managers of the farm clubs on which the boy is playing, or has played, add their notes to the voluminous file. By the time Krichell and Lee MacPhail have sifted the reports, they have a pretty fair idea as to whether "Mr. X" is ever going to be a Yankee or not.

A phase of scouting which is comparatively recent is that of scouting opponents. The Dodger "white paper" on Joe DiMaggio, which was turned over to the Giants when it was discovered that Brooklyn wasn't going to be in the World Series after all, caused a post-Series rhubarb when it was printed in October, 1951.

Just as it surprised recruits to the services to learn that there was so much paper-work to fighting a war, so will it surprise fans to learn of the amount of paper-work involved in operating a baseball system. And paper-work directly related to the playing of the game on the field is meant here, not auditing or bookkeeping.

When Stengel speaks pridefully of the organization, he does so with good cause for many of those who work toward the common end—a pennant in the Bronx—are interchangeable parts of the machine. Bill Skiff and Johnny Neun, for instance, can manage in the minors and act as general troubleshooters. They double as instructors, too, at the various rookie camps the Yankees run for their farm hands.

It is from the combined efforts of all these men, from Weiss to Jackie Farrell, whose principal job in 1951 was to keep Dizzy Dean's syntax untangled over TV, that the Yankees flourish. Men like Aaron Lanier, who has the prosaic job of auditing the books, and Jack White, who is in charge of the ticket sales, all play their parts in the organization.

One of the longest Yankee service records was that held by Charley McManus, whose title was superintendent of Yankee Stadium, from the park's opening until his death in 1953. Charley survived all the regimes of the modern Yanks and had many a strange experience, one of the most unusual of which was his meeting with the architect MacPhail brought to supervise the renovation of the Stadium.

"Mr. MacPhail introduced the man to me and said that some time after the World Series, he would come to my office in the Stadium," related Charley. "I was to put myself at his service and show him around the plant so he could decide where seats should be taken out or added.

"If I gave you a hundred guesses, you'd never guess what day he picked to come up to the Stadium and inspect the plant for the proposed changes—the morning of the Army-Notre Dame game in 1946!"

The Yankee organization faced a test in 1952, with Joe DiMaggio retired. No club can lose a player of Joe's calibre and fail to show it but on the other hand no other club has as able an organization as the Yanks have.

"Maybe we won't come up with another DiMag—how many such do you see in a lifetime?"—explained a member of the organization, "but our job is to see that Joe won't be missed too badly."

What kind of a job the Yankee organization has done in the past may be appreciated with the realization that the Yanks won pennants after Babe Ruth had gone, and after Lou Gehrig had gone. The chances are that they will go on winning them, without too long a gap between flags, for that's the way the organization is built.

CHAPTER II

"THE OL' PERFESSER"
(Casey Stengel)

BY TOM MEANY,
WITH JERRY MITCHELL

It was chilly out on New York's sunlit Fifth Avenue that afternoon of October 12, 1948. There were some who thought they detected a hint of chill inside, too, in the Yankee offices high in the Squibb Building. Flashlight bulbs and questions were popped in the order named as Charles Dillon Stengel did his very best to convince the assemblage of press and radio interviewers that managing the Yankees was precisely the task he had been fitting himself for during his four decades in organized baseball.

Stengel had come back to the majors after five years in the minors. He had come back to the biggest, most lush job in all baseball. Always popular with the writers of the metropolitan area during his playing career as a Giant and as coach and manager with the Dodgers, Casey looked for some friendly faces among the crowd. There were fewer than he had anticipated. Many of those who had been close to Stengel when he was a player and manager in the National League had moved on from the baseball beat to daily columns, or in some cases, had left the sports pages and the newspaper profession entirely. Some had died. . . .

Even so, Stengel should have had a more enthusiastic reception. He was mystified at the general attitude which, while not hostile, was definitely skeptical. He had been out at Oakland, winning a pennant and a Pacific Coast League playoff, when Bucky Harris had been relieved of his position as manager of the Yankees.

Harris was greatly respected by the writers who traveled with, or wrote about, the Yankees. He took charge in 1947, after a tumultuous season which had seen the impetuous Larry MacPhail employ a total of three managers—Joe McCarthy, Bill Dickey, and Johnny Neun. A job Harris coveted more than any other in baseball had been offered to him within a month after he had been named manager of the Yanks. The post was that of general manager of Detroit, but Harris explained that he had given his word to MacPhail that he would manage the Yanks.

In that first season, the Yanks under Harris won a pennant and a World Series. In his second year, Bucky brought the Yanks to within two games of the pennant. The day after the season ended, he was unceremoniously fired! He was fired, in fact, while the American League still was excited over the Red Sox-Cleveland playoff game, the first in its history.

The writers resented the firing of Harris and they resented its timing, since it came between the playoff game and the World Series, which meant that it got a minimum of discussion in the sports pages. As a consequence, they were not disposed to look kindly on Bucky's successor, whomever he might be. In the selection of Stengel, they suspected a plot to soften them up because of Casey's known popularity. He was resented, not because he was Stengel but because he was Bucky's successor.

Stengel, a shrewd operator, sensed the attitude. He did not take long to discover the reason for it. He set about to alleviate it by playing straight. He didn't clown. He made no specious claims. He buttered up the writers and told them they knew more about the Yankee situation than he did. He'd have to withhold comment until he reached St. Petersburg and saw what sort of hand he had been dealt.

Let's go now to the Biltmore Hotel in New York on the night of October 9, 1949, slightly less than a year after the frigid press conference on Fifth Avenue. Flash bulbs were popping again and so were champagne corks—but no questions. There wasn't any need to ask questions now, for the Yankees had won the pennant. They had won it gloriously by taking two straight from Boston on the last two days of the season, and they had beaten Brooklyn four out of five in a World Series triumph which assumed the proportions of a rout.

At the height of the hilarity, a reporter made his way to Stengel's side. He had been with Casey 15 years before when Stengel fought to keep the Dodgers out of the second division and out of the hands of the banks. He had finished the last half of the 1949 season with the Yanks when it seemed that the team was held together by baling wire.

The reporter shook Stengel's hand. "Congratulations, Case," he said simply. "I knew you when, and I've waited a long time for a night like this."

"It was a long, rough road at that, wasn't it?" remarked Stengel.

15

"Like mining hard coal with a toothpick," agreed the writer.

If winning his first World Championship was as difficult as mining hard coal for Stengel, he soon got used to it for he came up with World Series triumphs in each of his first four seasons in the American League, sweeping the Phillies in four straight in 1950 and taking the Giants in four out of six in 1951 and outlasting the Dodgers in seven in 1952.

Stengel was a baseball "card" from the start. On the day he applied for a tryout as an outfielder with Kansas City, his own town, a drive caromed off a fence and bounced past him.

"Get those balls," yelled his manager, Danny Shay. "Learn how to play those angles!"

"Angles," snorted Casey, less than a year out of high school. "If I have to learn the angles, I'd better go down to Johnny Kling's pool hall!"

Instead he went to Kankakee, Illinois, of the Northern Association, and the league folded so completely that no records of the 1910 season remain. He finished the year with Maysville, Kentucky, in the Blue Grass League, astounding his mates with his antics the day he reported.

Casey would haul down a fly ball in practice, throw it into the infield, sail his glove ahead of him on the grass, and then slide into the mitt.

"He won't be with us very long," a veteran observed sourly.

"You mean he's going up to the big leagues?" someone asked.

"No," was the reply. "There's an institution here to take care of guys like that." And he pointed to the buildings of the State Insane Asylum overlooking the center-field fence.

"I was simply practicing four things at once," Casey says in explanation. "I was catching, running, throwing, and sliding. I fooled 'em, too, because two years later I was up there—in the big leagues, I mean, not the nut-house."

Stengel was playing for Montgomery, Alabama, in the Southern Association when Manager Johnny Dobbs broke the news of his sale to Brooklyn. He was packing one of those old-fashioned valises when Kid Elberfeld, the former major-league star then winding up his days with Montgomery, came over to his rooming house to wish him luck.

"That's a thousand-miler if the weather stays good," said Elberfeld, nodding toward the suitcase. "But if it rains, you'll find yourself holding nothing but a handle. You'd better buy yourself a good one."

Casey had gone two-and-a-half years to Western Dental College in Kansas City, hoping to become one of the world's few left-handed dentists. Most of the money he had earned in the minors had gone into his schooling, and he faced the necessity of buying $150 worth of instruments that winter. He thought twice about every dollar before spending it, and the $20 Elberfeld said a new bag would cost seemed an expensive luxury.

"You'll need that bag if you're going to be a real big-leaguer," said the Kid, "and don't worry, you will be. You won't come back here, so just forget about being a dentist."

The brash kid from the minors was somewhat subdued when he landed in New York with his new suitcase, $95 in cash, and instructions to report to the Dodgers at Washington Park, in darkest South Brooklyn, the next morning. A cabbie took him to the Hotel Langford, but he never left the lobby to explore the Great White Way. He was afraid he might not be able to find his way back.

He found Washington Park in the morning with the help of two elevated-, three street-car rides, and innumerable directions from strangers. The gate-tender let him in with misgivings.

"Go on down there to your right," he directed, "and you'd better be good."

Those were the days of the Daffiness Boys in Brooklyn, and the recruit got an early introduction to their quaint habits. A crap game was going on in one corner of the clubhouse and in another, two Dodgers were sharing a bucket of beer. Young Stengel was introduced around by Zack Wheat, the only one who noticed him. There wasn't a handshake and only a few grunts. He was finally invited to join the crap game. Thinking that might help make him one of the mob, he accepted. In no time he was practically bare of his modest roll. He looked up to find Bill Dahlen, the Brooklyn manager, beckoning.

"You a crapshooter or a ballplayer?" asked Dahlen. Casey assured him he was a ballplayer.

"Then get out of that game while you still have carfare!" shouted Dahlen. "Put on a uniform and get out on that field."

Stengel got another, bigger surprise when Dahlen told him he was the starting center-fielder. Hub Northern, the regular, was sick, the victim of a big Dodger clambake at Coney Island the night before.

The Dodgers were playing the Pittsburgh Pirates and young Stengel got three straight hits off Claude Hendrix, the league's leading pitcher. He also swiped two bases, with George Gibson, one of the stars of the league, doing the Pittsburgh catching. Hendrix was finally removed in favor of a left-

18

hander and Fred Clarke, the Pirate manager, yelled to Casey:

"All right phenom, let's see you cross over."

"I was cocky enough to do it," said Casey. "I went up there and batted righthanded and damned if I didn't get a base on balls."

Later the Dodgers moved over to the Polo Grounds for a series and Stengel hit three line drives that were caught. McGraw, coming out to the coaching box, stopped him after he was robbed for the third time. "I have to hand it to you kid," he said. "No doubt about it, you're the best hitter on the Brooklyn ball club."

"Gee, thanks Mr. McGraw," replied Stengel, pleased at being rated above such batters as Zack Wheat by such an authority.

"But remember," concluded McGraw, "we just had that wall built, so don't go running into it with that hard head." The Dodgers were a lively lot then, on and off the field. Casey was the leader of a group of six called "The Grumblers."

"We'd always wind up in the same place after a home game," recalls Stengel, "and start beefing about the umpires, the owners, Uncle Robbie's mistakes, and the world in general. 'Here come The Grumblers,' the bartender would yell as we entered."

One night, The Grumblers got into a scrap with some of the customers who were riding them about the game they had lost that afternoon. Word of the rhubarb reached the club officers and Charley Ebbets, the president, visited the dressing rooms and gave all the athletes a lecture including Uncle Wilbert Robinson, the manager. After Ebbets departed in high dudgeon, Robbie and Stengel happened to be alongside each other, walking out under the stands to the dugout.

"You and Jeff Pfeffer and the others weren't drinking as much as Ebbets claims, were you, Case, old boy?" asked Robbie.

"Course not," assented Stengel. "We only had four apiece."

"Just four glasses?" persisted Robbie.

"That's right, just four," replied Stengel.

"Bet the glasses were as big as cooking pots, though, weren't they?" guffawed Robbie as he continued on to the field.

For a shade over five years, Stengel could do no wrong in Brooklyn. With the patrons, he was the Dixie Walker of his day. Then he was traded to Pittsburgh and suddenly found he was a bum. Once he took off the Dodger uniform, he lost his halo with it.

When Stengel appeared at Ebbets Field with the Pirates, he was roundly hooted. He disappeared for a few minutes right after batting practice and came back to the bench with his customary grin and a big wink. "Watch me," he said to his mates.

As Stengel came to take his first turn at bat, he was greeted by a veritable cannonade of boos. The noise increased in volume as Casey stopped halfway to the plate, returned to the Pittsburgh bench, and picked up as many bats as he could carry, swinging them in wide threatening arcs. He discarded all but one and stepped into the batter's box. The hooting sounded like a convention of indignant owls.

With a great sense of timing, Stengel lifted his hand to umpire Cy Rigler and called time. Then he bowed low to the jeering multitude, doffed his cap, and out flew a sparrow. It was the first time in history, perhaps the only time, that a performer responded to the figurative bird with a literal one, and it has gone down in history as one of baseball's most colorful incidents.

Stengel was one of the better major leaguers for 12 years with the Dodgers, Pirates, Phils, Giants, and Braves. His gaudiest seasons, perhaps, were spent under McGraw, the Giants winning three straight pennants with Casey in the outfield.

In 1922, he achieved his major-league high as a batter, hitting a hot .368 after McGraw had obtained him from the Phillies for players valued at $75,000. He won two games with home runs in the 1923 World Series, the only games the Giants were able to take from the Yankees.

The first was an inside-the-park homer, and one of the most dramatic blows in World Series history. The teams were tied 4-4 going into the ninth inning of the first Series game ever played in Yankee Stadium when Stengel hit a Joe Bush pitch to deep left center with Bob Meusel, then the best throwing outfielder in baseball, in hot pursuit.

It was strictly Stengel's legs against Meusel's arm, and Casey's gams were not too spry. He had a bone bruise, too, and a piece of foam rubber was in the shoe to cushion the damaged heel. The rubber bit popped out as Stengel rounded second and he was a side-wheeler the rest of the way, under the misapprehension that he had lost a shoe. He made it, crossing the plate with limbs going in all directions just ahead of Meusel's throw.

The baseball journalists went to town. They had a lot of fun picturing old man Stengel being wheeled to the plate, where he tucked his flowing white beard into his baseball shirt, took off his spectacles, belted the ball, and then gasped his way around the bases.

Stengel had been courting Miss Edna Lawson of Glendale, California, with the help of phone calls and special-delivery carriers, and they hoped to be married that Fall. Edna's parents had never seen Casey, however, and there was a natural curiosity to meet her hero. They had followed his play all Summer long and could hardly wait to open the sports pages the morning after the first World Series game.

They read, among others, Damon Runyon's story. It began:

"This is the way old Casey Stengel ran yesterday afternoon running his home run home.

"This is the way old Casey Stengel ran running his home run home to a Giant victory by a score of 5 to 4 in the first game of the World Series of 1923.

"This is the way old Casey Stengel ran running his home run home when two were out in the ninth and the score was tied, and the ball still bounding inside the Yankee yard.

"This is the way—

"His mouth wide open.

"His warped old legs bending beneath him at every stride.

"His arms flying back and forth like those of a man swimming with a crawl stroke.

"His flanks heaving, his breath whistling, his head far back. Yankee infielders, passed by old Casey Stengel, as he was running his home run home, say Casey was muttering to himself, adjuring himself to greater speed as a jockey mutters to his horse in a race, saying: 'Go on Casey, go on.'

"The warped old legs, twisted and bent by many a year of baseball campaigning, just barely held out under old Casey Stengel until he reached the plate, running his home run home.

"Then he collapsed."

It was after Mr. Lawson had finished Runyon's piece that his proud daughter said:

"What do you think of my Casey now, Pop?"

Mr. Lawson slowly folded his paper, then shook his head. "You'll be lucky," he said, "if he lives to make the wedding."

Casey Stengel was born Charles Dillon Stengel in Kansas City, Missouri, July 30, 1891. His father was of German descent, his mother Irish. He isn't sure of the reason for his nickname, applied since his minor league days, saying it could have been fashioned because of K.C., the abbreviation of the name of his hometown. Then, again, "Casey at the Bat" was a popular rendition during his early playing days and the tag was hung on many a baseball performer.

There were no notable athletes in the family history and Casey's days after grammar school were mostly occupied with efforts to add to the family finances with odd jobs. In his last two years at Manual Training High School, he helped his father Louis and brother Grant operate a sprinkling cart.

"I just wasn't cut out to be a sprinkler, I guess," he says. "Anyway, I wasn't much good at it. The rest of the family did the work. You might say they carried me."

It is possible that dentistry lost an outstanding craftsman when Stengel later decided to drop his bicuspid snatchers for

23

a baseball bat, for he fast became a prize student at Western Dental College in Kansas City, which he entered after his exit from high school.

By that time, Stengel was receiving offers from more independent ball clubs than he thought existed. The big break was a tryout with the Kansas City club in the Spring of 1910.

The green youngster was recommended to the Kankakee club of the Northern Association, but he had hardly gotten to know the names of his teammates when the league collapsed in July. He caught on with the Maysville club of the Blue Grass League and hit .223 in the 69 games that remained of that season. The following year found him at Aurora, of the Wisconsin-Illinois League, and his .352 average there brought about his transfer to Montgomery of the Southern Association, a club then enjoying friendly relations with Brooklyn of the National League.

Montgomery shipped Stengel to Brooklyn in September of 1912 on the strength of a .290 batting average. He made good, hitting .316 in 17 games, and the following Spring began a career that was to include 12 major-league seasons, six with the Dodgers, one with the Pittsburgh Pirates, one with the Phillies, two with the Giants, and two with the Boston Braves. His major-league lifetime batting average was .284, and his mark for three World Series a notable .393.

Stengel has a gargoyle face with palm-leaf ears, a mighty nose, and a wide, expressive mouth. His hair has been heavily splashed with gray since the days when he managed the Dodgers with mortgage companies and a dozen directors looking over his shoulder. His hands are forever in action as he talks and that, of course, is what Casey is doing most of the time. Sometimes, in the middle of a story, one hand will stray to

24

his mouth and linger over it long enough to wipe out an entire sentence.

He is, despite a habit of answering some questions with a knowing wink and a way of telling stories by way of Kansas City, Toledo, Milwaukee, and numerous other points, an entertaining conversationalist. The wide detours Casey takes in every story are invariably as amusing as the story he originally started to relate.

Like most ballplayers, Stengel has always been a big beef-eater. Give him a thick steak medium-rare, a dish of sliced onions and tomatoes, and a bowl of hashed brown potatoes, and he's more than content. He's a plain ham-and-eggs, sunny-side-up man at breakfast, and often skips lunch. He's a stickler for seeing that his players get a good deal in hotel dining rooms on the road as a number of American League hotels, to whom he was a stranger, discovered.

When he managed the Dodgers, incidentally, Stengel had what he described as a sure-fire system for catching the after-hour cutups on the club. He never waited up in the lobby for them; he simply inspected their breakfast checks.

"You know that the guy who has orange juice, cereal, bacon and eggs, toast and coffee, or an order like that hasn't been up fooling around all night," says Casey. "It's those who order double tomato juice and black coffee who go out to mail letters at three o'clock in the morning."

Stengel has a mine of strange and amusing expressions. Spying a Brooklyn writer wearing a pair of bifocals as he scanned the paper one day, Casey said: "He looks like Ned from the Third Reader."

The awfulness of the talent available to him in Brooklyn was only too clear to the naked eye, but in Boston spectacles were prescribed for Casey for the first time. Peering at his batting order card through them, he looked just like Ned from the Third Reader himself.

He isn't too particular what is ordered as a social stimulant at any gathering, just so it is good, but his favorite drink is Scotch and soda. Frisch converted him to Martinis one awful season but he turns to that cocktail now only in desperation or in the middle of a long losing streak.

Stengel always has dressed conservatively. In the old days, he featured velour hats of various shades and in Winter months heavy overcoats with belted back. Now he's a snap-brim hat man, inclined to neatly cut topcoats. Suits lean heavily to double-breasted blues and grays, though he startled the Yankees for a while with a pair of russet slacks and a gray sports jacket one Summer.

In his clubhouse room after a game, Casey will sit for a few hours in his shorts, with a cigarette and a bottle of beer. He'll continue talking to writers, coaches, or whoever drops in while taking his shower, popping his head out of the stall occasionally to put over a point. His attire is likely to consist of a bath towel for another hour as he moves into and around the players' locker room, stopping to talk to Rizzuto, and others who like to take their time and talk the day's game over again and again.

Stengel is probably the only ballplayer to start his managerial career as president of the same team. This happened when the Boston Braves, with whom he wound up his major-league career as a player, bought the Worcester, Massachusetts, club of the Eastern League and installed him as both field and office head in 1925. He liked the dual job, but he liked the offer of a job managing Toledo of the American Association a lot more. So he took off his uniform, went up to the club office, sat in the president's chair, and fired himself as manager.

"Manager Charles Dillon Stengel is hereby and as of this date dismissed as manager of the Worcester, Eastern League, club. Signed, Charles Dillon Stengel, President, Worcester Baseball Club."

Thus read the letter, required by baseball law, which Stengel sent to the office of Judge Kenesaw Mountain Landis, then high commissioner of baseball. The Judge was popularly believed to have looked with disfavor on this bit of business, and the rumor spread that Stengel would not be allowed to work for a major-league club again.

The report delayed Brooklyn's acceptance of Casey as one of Max Carey's coaching aides when he applied for the job in 1932. The grapevine proved false, however, and he returned to his first major-league love, the Dodgers.

The Brooklyn directors, beset as usual by money troubles, decided after two sorry seasons that it would be cheaper to hire a new manager than a new ball club. Carey's contract had a year to go, but they dropped him and put the question to Stengel.

Loyalty has always been one of Casey's outstanding qualities. He showed it when Bob Quinn, then general manager of the Dodgers, asked him to succeed Carey. He wouldn't agree to sign unless assured that Max was through in Brooklyn whether he took the job or not, and that Carey would be fully paid for the remaining year of his contract.

When he managed the Dodgers, Van Lingle Mungo, the big fastball pitcher, was practically the only professional on the team. The rest were worn veterans unwanted by other clubs and youngsters with little experience and often less abil-ity, and an occasional character who was carried on the payroll only at the insistence of one of the club directors. Bolstering deals couldn't be made because Brooklyn had no players worth offering to other clubs, and there wasn't enough money avail-able to buy promising athletes from the minors.

The directors included a hat manufacturer whose knowl-edge of baseball would hardly fill one of his own beanies, a movie executive who spent most of his time, naturally, in Hollywood, and another who once pitched for Yale and wouldn't let anyone forget it. In fact, the ex-Yale pitcher used to tell the Brooklyn pitchers, young and old, what was wrong with their deliveries.

Some of the most bizarre of the Brooklyns held forth dur-ing Stengel's regime. They somehow managed to pick up an outfielder one winter by the name of Oscar (The Ox) Eck-hardt, who had led the Pacific Coast League in hitting the previous season (1935).

Great things were predicted for the Ox, who had etab-lished high batting marks in a number of other seasons also, once leading the Texas League. They began to worry, how-ever, when Eckhardt wasn't present when camp opened. Fran-tic wires were sent and finally came an answer. Eckhardt agreed to report. The telegram said, "Reserve room for two." The club figured Eckhardt wanted to bring his wife to camp, a practice usually frowned upon and practically unheard of in the case of a rookie. There was such need of better hitting on the Dodgers of that day, however, that they decided to humor their phenom. So they wired back that a room for two would be reserved and to please hurry.

Stengel and an assortment of directors were in the lobby

later that week when the rookie walked in to register. There was no wife in sight. Instead was an over-sized St. Bernard on a leash. The Ox gravely explained that he had always taken his dog to training camp in the minors and that he figured it would be even more of a treat to his pet to see a major-league camp!

Like almost every Brooklyn acquisition of that period, Eckhardt proved a complete flop. After the first 16 games of the season, in which he batted only .119, he was back in the minors again.

That was the Spring, too, that Frenchy Bordagaray reported from his California home with a mustache and a full-blown goatee. Frenchy had been a clean-shaven outfielder with frisky feet and a habit of running against stop signals and the strongest throwing arms the season before. This time he apparently figured something new had to be added.

Stengel went along with him for the sake of the publicity to be gained by such stories from training camp, something that got extra consideration in Brooklyn because of the poor quality of the baseball offered. After the first week of play, however, it was announced that while the mustache would remain, the goatee had to go.

"He runs faster without it," explained Stengel. "Besides, he was always tempted to try and trap ground balls in the goatee. He has enough trouble fielding grounders with his hands."

Mungo was about the only Dodger, aside from the exercising clubowners, who rated one of the better uniforms each Spring. The others went around in patch-work suits that had to be kept under constant repair by Babe Hamberger, a stout, industrious, and carefree worker who was known as Casey

Stengel's meatball. The Babe was the club's man-of-all-work and still is, but the days are gone when he has to set up a sewing machine outside the clubhouse, as he did that Spring in Orlando, Florida, to put old uniforms together. Today the Dodgers get them wholesale. . . .

Stengel, manfully conniving to keep the Dodgers safe from foreclosure, invariably made Mungo his Sunday pitcher, since Van's fast ball and his strikeout skill did much to make the fans forget what a really incompetent team the Dodgers were. It didn't work out too well for Mungo, because he usually drew the other team's ace pitcher. It was a pitching duel, all right, but eventually somebody booted one behind Van and the show was over.

Days of glory were few and far between for Stengel as a Brooklyn manager, but he did wind up his first season on the job as the borough's favorite son.

Bill Terry had won the pennant and World Series in 1933, his first full season as John McGraw's successor, and he was both proud and talkative when he returned to New York for the Winter meetings. At one of them, someone asked him what he thought of Brooklyn's prospects for 1934.

"Brooklyn?" asked Terry. "Is Brooklyn still in the league?"

The crack was regarded as the dirtiest in decades in Brooklyn and the frequent repetition of it by visiting Giant fans at Ebbets Field led to some of the goriest grandstand scraps of the season. The Dodger faithful were entitled to consider matters even, however, when their heroes went up to the Polo Grounds on the last two days of the season and knocked the Giants out of a possible pennant.

The Giants had all but dissipated a huge lead over the

St. Louis Cardinals when the Dodgers arrived on the scene. After the Brooks won the final Sunday game, which gave the pennant to the Cards, it took Stengel more than four hours to reach his Brooklyn hotel. Triumphant Dodger fans, who had dotted the Polo Grounds with banners reading: "Is Brooklyn Still in the League? And How!" carried him on their shoulders from the clubhouse exit down into the subway where they decked the trains with their banners. The train went from the Polo Grounds to Coney Island, back to the Polo Grounds, then to Brooklyn again, before Casey finally made his escape at Borough Hall.

Eventually adversity got the better of Mungo's good nature and he began to pour more than fastballs. He also started to brood after every defeat. Following a particularly rough one in Pittsburgh, he unloaded his woes, real and imaginary, on a baseball writer who chanced to hit the same thirst parlor. Finally, he mumbled that by golly he had a mind to jump the club and return to Brooklyn where he could ask for a better deal from "Judge" Steve McKeever, the club president.

The writer leaped at the chance to sew up an exclusive story. He got tickets on the midnight plane for New York for Mungo and himself, after filing the story of Van's rebellion. In the meantime, the club secretary heard of the plan and begged the pitcher not to go. He was still begging when the writer returned, showed Mungo the tickets, and told Van he'd have to go through with it since the story was already in the papers.

The distraught secretary rushed to the hotel to get help from Stengel. He found Casey sitting in a darkened room with his head in his hands, as disconsolate as Mungo.

"No use of me trying to talk him out of it," Casey answered when the secretary asked for help. "He wouldn't listen, the shape he's in. Let him go. We can lose with him or without him."

The needler and the rebel eventually arrived in Brooklyn where they rushed to McKeever. On any other club, the pitcher would have been severely fined and censured and the manager told that the directorate was firmly behind him, but nothing came of the incident, except what amounted to a short vacation with pay for Mungo.

However, the affair was believed to have had a lot to do with the decision to buy up Stengel's contract after the season. They paid him off for 1937 during the 1936 World Series, thus providing some off-the-field entertainment for the assembled baseball men, most of whom had experience with the daffy doings of the Dodger directorate.

Since Max Carey, the man Casey succeeded, had been paid in full for *not* managing the club in 1934, and Burleigh Grimes went on the payroll as the actual 1937 leader, the poor but slap-happy Dodgers set some sort of a record by paying six managerial salaries over a four-year span.

The release of Stengel cost the Dodgers a lot of newspaper friends. Casey's pals among the press arranged a fancy banquet at the Hotel New Yorker in his honor after the World Series and more than 200 attended, most of them demanding the toastmaster's permission for a few minutes' time in which to personally denounce the Brooklyn directors.

It was supposed to be strictly a newspapermen's affair, but the Yankees, who even then felt fond of Stengel, pleaded for the right to attend. Thus, General Manager George Weiss, who 12 years later was to sign Casey as manager of the Yanks, sat on the dais, along with manager Joe McCarthy. Elsewhere

32

in the crowded room were Yankee scouts Joe Devine, Harry Hesse, Bill Essick, Paul Krichell, and Johnny Nee.

After his year of exile, Casey signed to manage the Boston Braves for Bob Quinn, for whom he had worked in Brooklyn and who had moved on to become general manager in Boston. In Brooklyn he had finished sixth, fifth, and seventh in that order. In six Boston seasons, he failed to make the first division. He was fifth the first year, then seventh four years in a row, and finally sixth in his last year.

The record wasn't good, but neither was the ball club. Stengel advanced the club $43,000 of his own money and talked Max Meyer, an old Brooklyn friend, into buying into the team. Meyer was a manufacturer of imitation pearls. What they needed in Boston was someone who could make silk purses out of sow's ears.

During Casey's years there, the club acquired many relics but few good, young players who could help lift the club to first division heights. Injuries of all sorts plagued him. His first season had hardly begun when catcher Al Lopez suffered a badly mashed finger; pitcher Lefty Shoffner lost his appendix; Danny MacFayden, another pitcher, had his hand broken by a line drive; Ray Mueller, another catcher, broke a finger; and outfielder Gene Moore had to have a knee operation.

"They have courage all right," Casey said of his boys at the time. "All you have to do is tape 'em together."

Just before the 1943 season, Stengel's sixth with the Braves, opened, Casey was crossing the street near Boston's Hotel Kenmore. It was a drizzling, foggy night and Casey, with his overcoat wrapped up around his face, never saw the auto which hit him. He suffered a badly broken leg and was two months in the hospital before he could walk again. In his absence, the Braves' coaches, Bob Coleman and George Kelly, ran the club.

Casey's wife, caring for an invalid mother in California, phoned when she heard the news and said she'd rush East.

"Don't come," said Casey, "unless you know how to set a broken leg."

Stengel couldn't stand listening to the broadcasts of the Braves' games. When the club left for a long Western trip, he said to Kelly; "When you get back, I'll be either out of the hospital or out of my mind!"

Casey was comic relief for Boston after quiet Bill Mc-Kechnie. As Harold Kaese, the Boston sportswriter, observed in his splendid history of the Braves:* "For writers following the club, it was more fun losing with Stengel than winning with a hundred other managers they could name. Unfortunately, Boston fans did not have the benefit of Stengel's company."

Not all the critics stayed on his side, however. In fact Dave Egan, the able Boston sports critic, called on the people to honor the driver who had run Stengel down (and thus deprived the Braves of his services as manager for more than two months) as "the man who had done the most for baseball in Boston in 1943."

The best Stengel got out of the Braves was the $43,000 he loaned the club in 1938. This maintained Stengel's record, both as being one of the few managers with money to invest in a ball club and as one of the few able to get it back again. He had loaned his owners money in Toledo in 1929 and had been repaid.

Stengel did even better on an investment he made out-

* *The Boston Braves*, G. P. Putnam's Sons, 1948.

side of baseball. Randy Moore, an outfielder from Lancaster, Texas, suggested that they pool their pennies and go after some possible oil property in East Texas, where a mild boom was starting. With Stengel and Moore went Van Mungo, catcher Al Lopez, and Johnny Cooney. Oil spouted in 1941 and is still flowing.

"It's nothing sensational, though," says Casey, always shy in talking about his investments, which also include a Glendale, California, theatre and a hotel in the same city. "The oil well is something like an annuity. It pays a steady income but not a big one."

Unfortunately, Stengel's jests began to sound like hollow echoes in the darkened confines of the second division. There were few protests when a group composed of Lou Perini, Guido Rugo, and Joseph Maney purchased the club from the other members of the syndicate that had owned the Braves since 1941. For a while it looked as though Casey's friend Meyer and elder statesman Bob Quinn would be the top bidders but the trio of building contractors who became known as the Three Little Steam Shovels won out. They said Stengel, who had more than once suggested that they stick to their tools and not interfere in his management of the club, would not be rehired.

The 1944 season opened with Stengel out of work. But he did not stay out for long. When the Chicago Cubs called Charley Grimm back from their Milwaukee farm club in the American Association in early May of that season to manage the club again, Charley suggested Stengel for the Milwaukee job.

Bill Veeck, at that time titular head of the Milwaukee

club, was then otherwise engaged as a Marine in the South Pacific. The news that the American Association was still operating, despite the war, came as a surprise to him. But the announcement of Stengel's appointment was a shock.

Veeck began to bombard the Milwaukee office with scorching letters. The first one said:

"Gentlemen: I learned an hour ago the identity of our new manager. I've waited an hour to write this, hoping to cool off. So far it hasn't been too successful. To say that I'm very disappointed is putting it mildly.

"I'd like to have a complete explanation of where Stengel came from. Who suggested him? Who hired him? For how much and for how long? I don't want anything to do with Stengel, nor do I want him to have anything to do with anything I have a voice in.

"I will now proceed to elucidate the above:

"First, Stengel has never managed a winner. In my humble opinion, he is a poor manager.

"Second, he has been closely connected with Bob Quinn and the operation of the Boston Braves. This in itself is enough to damn him.

"Third, I don't believe that Stengel is a good judge of ballplayers so can be of no value to us in amassing future clubs.

"Fourth, from what I know of Stengel he is tight-fisted and this will not prove acceptable.

"Fifth, from my observation, Stengel is mentally a second-division major-leaguer. That is, he is entirely satisfied with a mediocre ball club as long as Stengel and his alleged wit are appreciated.

"Sixth, I have no confidence in his ability and rather than

be continuously worried, I'd rather dispose of the whole damn thing.

"Seventh, Stengel doesn't fit in at all with the future—and I'm looking, as usual, for the long haul.

"If these aren't reasons enough, I don't like him and want no part of him. Starting now . . . If Stengel has an iron-clad contract and it will be expensive to break I guess that we'll have to be stuck with him. If not, replace him immediately with Ivy Griffin."

Mickey Heath, Milwaukee vice-president, and other officials hastened to write Veeck that the Brewers were running away with the league, that Stengel was popular with the fans, that it would be dangerous to fire him. Reluctantly, with letters taking more than two weeks each way, Veeck agreed that Stengel could stay for the season—but no more!

As late as May 26 he was still blasting Stengel in his letters from various Pacific atolls.

"I guess I'm over my surprise about Stengel," he penned. "I'm still of the same opinion as to his ultimate value, but the press seems to have taken to him and with the club doing well he should be OK until the season ends."

Stengel, himself, never heard from Veeck. When Heath reminded Bill of this on August 27, when the American Association pennant had been all but wrapped up, Bill replied: "Possibly you are right. However, I still contend that he is a poor manager."

The Brewers won the flag by seven games. It was Casey's second flag in the American Association, since he had been the boss when Toledo won its only pennant in 1927. He was, as usual, the life of the party when the club staged a victory celebration the night the pennant was clinched. Everybody in the room seemed to be having a hilarious time with the exception of Heath, who stood glumly in a corner.

"What's the matter, Mickey?" asked R. G. Lynch, the sports editor of the Milwaukee *Journal*. "You won the pennant, remember?"

"Yeah, we won the pennant," he replied. "But how am I going to tell that guy"—indicating Stengel—"that he won't be back next year?"

"Do you want me to tell him?" asked Lynch.

"Will you?" said Heath, his face lighting with relief. "Will you?"

Stengel caught on fast when Lynch went to his hotel room the next afternoon and broke the news. "Listen, you can put in the paper that I will not be back next year," he said. "I made it plain to Charley Grimm when I took the job that it was just as a favor to him for one season, and that he would have to get someone else for next year. My leg bothers me more than I care to admit. I shouldn't have managed this year. I like the town, and the ball club is going to be a good one, but I've got to think about myself."

Lynch later wrote Veeck, telling him, in effect, that he should be ashamed of himself. He suggested that Veeck write Stengel. Veeck had by this time been evacuated from Bougainville in the Pacific with the foot injury which later necessitated amputation, and was getting his mail in a service hospital at Corona, California. He immediately wrote Stengel, congratulated him on a great job, and begged Casey to visit him in the hospital if he possibly could do so. Casey did and they hit it off like two old college chums.

Late that November, a New York sportswriter received

38

a surprise long distance call from Veeck, still in the hospital but anxious to move again in baseball. After an exchange of pleasantries, Veeck came right to the point. He had, it seems, read of the death a few days previously, of Leo Bondy, treasurer of the New York Giants, and he wondered if that would make any change in the status of the club. Could they now be purchased?

Veeck was told that although Bondy had been generally considered the man who held the Giants' purse strings, he owned no stock in the club and that it was improbable that it would be allowed to pass from the control of the Stoneham family.

"Too bad," said Bill, philosophically, "because I'd like to buy it if the price was right. And you know who I'd put in as manager, don't you?"

"Who?" asked the writer.

"Your old friend Casey Stengel," replied Veeck. "He's my man!"

It was Stengel's plan to stay out of baseball in 1945 and he looked forward to enjoying daily dips in the swimming pool behind his new Italian-style mansion in Glendale, California. Such was his plan, that is, until he attended the Winter baseball meetings for old times' sake and there met Weiss, who was looking for a manager for the Yankees' Kansas City farm.

Weiss and Casey were old friends, their companionship dating back to the latter's days as manager and president of the Worcester club in 1925. Weiss was then the young owner of the New Haven team in the same Eastern League and had proposed, at one time, that they join forces and move the franchise to Providence with Casey serving as manager. The plot never jelled and Stengel moved on to boss Toledo.

Weiss backed Stengel into a corner every night of the meeting and finally got his man to agree to the Kansas City job. But Casey wasn't nearly as successful as at Milwaukee the year before, finishing seventh. However, Yankee officials admitted that Casey had the use of the poorest crop of Yankee farmhands in many years.

The years and the bad ballplayers were beginning to get Stengel down. Once again he made a post-season decision to stay out of the game, at least for a year. But back on the Coast another old friend, Brick Laws, owner of the Oakland Pacific Coast League club, began to beg him to manage the club.

Like Weiss, Laws finally won his man over. What sold Stengel was the fact that he would be fairly close to home at all times, with the ball game almost in his back yard when the Oaks invaded Los Angeles and Hollywood. He liked the idea, too, of the long seven-game series in vogue in the league. He looked forward to a nice Summer and that's just what he got. He enjoyed three in a row, in fact, with Oakland getting into the play-offs the first two years and then winning the club's first pennant since 1921, as well as the play-offs, in 1948.

With the announcement of the dismissal of Bucky Harris in New York reports of candidates for the Yankee job began to pop wherever baseball men gathered in Boston, where the World Series between the Cleveland Indians and Boston Braves was about to start. Al Simmons, a favorite of Dan Topping's, was the man, said some. Others whispered that it would be Tommy Henrich, Joe DiMaggio, Milkman Jim Turner, who had been managing for the Yankees in the minors, Luke

40

Sewell, the former manager of the St. Louis Browns, Bill Mc-
Kechnie, a coach for the Cleveland Indians, or Bill Terry,
former boss of the Giants. Those who knew how close Weiss
and Stengel were put their bets on Casey. They won October
12 with the announcement that he had been signed to a two-
year contract.

Weiss had followed Stengel's work at Oakland with in-
creasing interest all Summer. Del Webb, one of the Yankee
owners and another old acquaintance of Casey's had also
watched many an Oakland game when business took him to
the Coast. When a change in managers was decided, Weiss
sought still more information from Joe Devine, who scouted
the Pacific Coast territory for the Yanks, and the latter had
only the highest praise for Stengel's work.

They first approached Stengel through long-distance calls
while his Oakland club was busy in the play-offs. He tabled
the matter for the time being. But after the Oaks had won, he
discussed the offer with his owner, Brick Laws. The two then
flew to New York for a secret meeting with Weiss, Webb, and
Topping. After several thousand words, most of them spoken
by Casey, the Yankees had signed their new manager.

"I've always been on friendly terms with Casey," said
Weiss afterwards, "and Del Webb knew him fairly well from
the Coast. But he didn't get this job through friendship. The
Yankees represent an investment of perhaps two or three
million dollars. They don't hand out jobs like that because
they like your company. Stengel got the job because the Yankees think he can produce for them."

When the Yankees' Spring training started in Florida,
there was a somewhat different Stengel from those sad-sack
days in Brooklyn and Boston. As he put it later in the season:

41

"Clowning around is all right when you have a second-division club. It helps create some interest when you're going bad, and it gives the boys something to write about besides losing streaks, and bad players. But you don't have to always leave them laughing when you're up there. . . . And I mean to be up there."

He knew it would be a tough job, calling for serious stuff. He was managing a club that had been run by such acknowledged masters as Miller Huggins and Joe McCarthy, a club with a vast tradition of triumph. There were many problems, including one of discipline for some athletes who had not taken their jobs too seriously the year before. He had only to read the papers to learn that he was inheriting a fading team and a fading Joe DiMaggio, the best ballplayer in the business.

Stengel laid it right on the line for the Yankees, young and old, when camp opened. "I didn't ask for this job," he said. "They came to me. I took it and I know I have a job to do. I'm going to act like a Yankee and I want you to do the same. You're all old enough to know how to behave. I'll expect you to keep in condition. Above all, no group drinking."

The manner in which Stengel handled his problems, including some that weren't anticipated, helped create a new respect for him. The players were properly impressed, not only with their individual treatment, but by the way Casey acted when he learned that he wouldn't have the services of DiMaggio, a cripple again with a damaged heel.

Like DiMaggio, Phil Rizzuto had been plagued by injury. A shoulder ailment had threatened to ruin his career as a top-flight shortstop, and no one knew how he would be able to play. People who had been around the Yankees longer than

Casey advised him to ride Rizzuto into action early, so that the shortstop might get rid of his shoulder soreness by hard work from the start. Casey listened as always, winked, and then did it the other, wiser way.

"You've been around, Phil," he told Rizzuto, "and you know yourself best. Take your time, get into shape your own way. Come out mornings if you feel like it, or work out anywhere and however you want. I won't put you in the lineup until you tell me okay."

Stengel had been briefed on the faults and accomplishments of all the Yankees before getting to camp. There he digested further information supplied by his coaches, Frankie Crosetti, Jim Turner, and Bill Dickey. Then he began to find things out for himself. . . .

He was credited with introducing the two-platoon system to the major leagues last season. As a matter of fact, Casey had beaten the Army's Earl Blaik and everyone else to it in his last two years at Oakland.

With the Yankees, Stengel played Jerry Coleman at second base part of the time, resting the youngster now and then to use the veteran Snuffy Stirnweiss. Billy Johnson was the third baseman against lefthanded pitching, Bobby Brown the man when righthanders were working. Casey alternated Charley Keller, Cliff Mapes, Johnny Lindell, Gene Woodling, and Hank Bauer in the outfield. Only DiMaggio, when he was able to play, Henrich, and Rizzuto were fixtures against all type of pitchers.

Stengel introduced a tandem pitching gimmick, too, with Allie Reynolds as the starter and Joe Page the finisher of most of Reynolds' starts.

It was apparent in Spring training that Joe DiMaggio

would be lost for at least half the season. But the Yankees, un-discouraged, grabbed the lead when play began and were never out of it until a week before the finish, when the Boston Red Sox pulled even and then moved a game in front.

Stengel rallied his forces, refused to lose faith in Joe Page, who had been whipped in four previous relief appearances, and beat back the Bostons the only way it was possible—by winning the last two games of the season.

Most of the year it seemed certain that if the Yankees won, they would have to play the World Series in the recreation hall of Lenox Hill Hospital, where ailing and damaged ath-letes had been shipped from the Stadium almost every day. They had to survive 76 cases of injury and illness before re-gaining the championship of the world.

They were still in first place in June, but the Red Sox were edging closer and there was a three-game series with them in Boston coming up. DiMaggio, still weak from the time spent on crutches, had taken some brief outfield workouts. He sud-denly asked Stengel to try him out in a night exhibition game with the Giants.

"Stengel is a wonderful and understanding fellow," said DiMag. "All he said to me was: 'Okay, when you've got enough, let me know.' He started looking at me in the fifth inning and every inning thereafter, but I played it through. After the game I told him: 'My foot held up pretty good, Casey. I might be ready for you in Boston.' 'You're the boss,' he answered."

DiMaggio beat the Red Sox practically by himself, hit-ting four home runs in the three days. The Sox were a long time recovering from that blow.

It had taken restraint and good judgment for a manager

in Stengel's spot not to try and use DiMag as a pinch-hitter or part-time performer before the man was in good working order. He knew Joe wanted to be in there just as much as he wanted DiMaggio in there. But he wisely waited the man's own nod rather than risk ruining his career for a few pinch-hits. He followed the same system when DiMaggio broke down again later on, and when the slugger suffered an attack of virus pneumonia in the all-important final weeks of the race.

Stengel is believed to have introduced the complimentary phrase "He's an old pro!" into baseball. In 1949, he used it often in speaking of Tommy Henrich, the veteran whose play at first base and in the outfield, even when crippled, had so much to do with the Yankees' winning fight. Henrich suffered a broken toe and came back a few days later to play anyway with a hole cut in his shoe. Later in Chicago, he smashed his vertebra against a concrete outfield wall trying to make a catch and some authorities predicted the end of his career. But Tommy was back to aid the club in its stretch drive with the help of a corset and more than the usual allotment of intestinal fortitude.

To Henrich, Stengel was a pleasant surprise. "I had heard plenty about him, of course," said the veteran, "but most of it was just funny stuff. Last season I learned to appreciate him as a manager. He did a wonderful job with us. I don't know of any manager who could have done a better one. I rank him right up there with Joe McCarthy—and you know what I've always thought of Joe."

The Yankees' victory by four games to one in the World Series with the Dodgers was a fitting climax to Stengel's comeback. But when it was over, he brushed aside applause to praise his players and coaches and the Yankee organization. "It's the greatest in baseball," he said. "I worked for it before, finished in the soup at Kansas City, and left voluntarily. When they picked me last winter, they picked me for reasons that they knew better than I did, or better than I know now.

"It wasn't any accident that we won, and it wasn't any accident that I was at last a winning manager. Whenever we lost one of our stars, somebody else always popped up to do the job until we could get the star back. When I decided to use Coleman at second base, for example, the Yankees knew all about him and he knew all about second base.

"The scouts knew the players they were sending up and what was required of the players they sent up. It was the organization that won, not me."

CHAPTER III

THE YANKEE CLIPPER
(Joe DiMaggio)

BY TOM MEANY

When Joe DiMaggio faced a battery of television cameras, photographers, reporters and interested bystanders in the Yankee offices on December 11, 1951, and announced that he was through as an active player, he surprised a lot of people but he really didn't shock anybody.

The end of the trail had been looming for Joe all through the season. His biggest value to the Yankees was that he was Joe DiMaggio, wearing No. 5, playing center field and batting clean-up. He wasn't the old Joe, by any means. He couldn't get around on the ball, fast balls fooled his reflexes and he couldn't throw or cover the ground as he once did. Nevertheless, just being DiMaggio, he looked good out there; the Yankees felt better with him, and the opposition still worried about him.

When the Yanks squared off with Leo Durocher's amazing Giants in the World Series, Joe was held hitless on his first dozen trips to the plate. It wasn't until the fourth game, against Sal Maglie at the Polo Grounds, that the Clipper began to pull the ball. He hit a sharp single to left on his second trip, and a homer into the upper left field seats with a man on on his third trip. He hit in each of the next two games and wound up with a Series average of .261.

It was only natural that the writing boys should let themselves go when DiMaggio called it a career. There were some fine columns written and Arthur Daley of the *New York Times* did one of the most interesting, for he put his finger on what probably was the straw which tipped the scales—the publication in *Life* of the scouting report Andy High had turned in on the Yanks. It was meant to be used by the Dodgers against the Yanks but fate decided that the Brooks weren't to make the Series, so High's report was turned over to his fellow National Leaguers.

The report, of course, was supposed to be top-secret. Garry Schumacher, promotional director of the Giants and a lifelong friend of High's, had obtained it. When Durocher reported what a help it had been, mention was made of High's generosity but nothing of the contents of the report.

Clay Felker, an enterprising young man connected with the Giant radio broadcasts, finally wangled a copy of the report from the Dodgers and sold it to *Life* for a fat fee, plus a job in the magazine's sports department.

Everybody hollered bloody murder, the Giants, Dodgers and Yanks, together. The report had this to say about DiMaggio: "He can't stop quickly and throw hard. . . . You can take the extra base on him. . . . He can't run and won't bunt. . . . His reflexes are very slow and he can't pull a good fast ball at all."

As Daley said, "This must have cut him to the quick." It did. Joe wasn't going to take that sort of criticism—not even for $100,000 a year.

Things were pretty hilarious in the Yankee dressing room after the second game of the 1947 World Series. The Dodgers had been easy in the first two games and the general belief was that there would be no more baseball in Yankee Stadium that fall. The three games in Ebbets Field should wind it up. Maybe, even, three wouldn't be necessary. It could be wound up in two, in the traditional four-game sweep of the Bronx Bombers.

Relaxed and pleased, but not exactly hilarious, Joe Di-Maggio sprawled on a stool in front of his locker, the second from the last on the right hand side. He had loosened his baseball trousers and unbuttoned his blouse. He was drawing lazily and contentedly on a cigarette, the picture of a man who was taking his ease after a job well done. The shower could wait.

One of the reporters in the little knot clustered around DiMaggio wanted to know if he had any explanation for the troubles which had beset the Dodgers' Pete Reiser in center field that afternoon. Pete, and the rival left fielders, Gene Hermanski of the Dodgers and Johnny Lindell, seemed bedeviled by the sun.

Quickly DiMag went to the rescue of his brother outfielders, explaining that late in the fall afternoons the shadows in Yankee Stadium were very tricky and that the situation was complicated with a big crowd, since the combined smoke from sixty or seventy thousand fans threw a haze before the stands which gave the left and center fielders a difficult background.

Bob Cooke, of the New York *Herald Tribune,* took this as a logical explanation for the troubles of Reiser, Hermanski and Lindell but a thought struck him. He said:

"Well, Joe, how about yourself? Doesn't this haze and tricky background bother you?"

DiMaggio looked at Cooke almost without expression. He waited a second or two and then said, grinningly, "Bob, you aren't going to start worrying about the 'old boy' now, are you?"

It was the first time, perhaps the only time, anybody ever heard DiMaggio refer to himself in the third person. "I realized then," said Cooke in retelling the story, "that Joe had been explaining about the hazards the background presented to *ordinary* outfielders. It never even occurred to him that he might have trouble out there."

It may seem pointless to bring in an anecdote about DiMaggio's fielding skill but Joe was the sort of ball player you can't discuss in sections. He was *all* ball player and his fielding was as much a part of him as his hitting or his base running or his spirit. He was a perfectionist, albeit a very human one.

DiMaggio had no desire to see Reiser, or any ball player, criticized for defensive lapses which could be excused. He could excuse those lapses but, of course, he couldn't excuse them in himself. In fact, he never even thought about the possibility of a lapse and, therefore, of the need of an excuse for one.

DiMaggio was one of baseball's picture hitters. He employed a wide open stance, standing well back in the box, feet planted firmly and well apart. His stride was short, five or six inches, and he did a minimum of preliminary bat-waggling. His right elbow was fairly close to his side, the bat was held at the extreme end and rested on his right shoulder. If Joe were to take the same stance, discard his bat and extend his left arm straight out, he would look like an old boxing print of John L. Sullivan with the right hand cocked close to his breast.

The stance is the same one Joe used when he was a preteen-age kid, playing on the old Horse Lot of San Francisco. The only advice the Clipper ever received on batting was a tip or two from Lefty O'Doul, when the latter was managing the Seals just before Joe came to the majors. And such tips did not alter his stance but consisted of advice on how to pull the ball. Since DiMaggio batted with his feet apart, he pulled almost every pitch to left field.

A right-handed pull-hitter such as DiMaggio is at a disadvantage at Yankee Stadium, which was custom-built for Babe Ruth and the many left-handed pull-hitters the Yanks have had since. Once in a great while, Joe hit to right field but most of his hits into that territory were the result of late timing, with only a few being deliberately placed to right.

"I'm paid to hit the long ball," DiMaggio explained one time, "and I can hit the long ball only to left. If I tried to hit to right, I'd probably lose the groove of my swing and wind up being able to hit to neither field."

DiMaggio's stance made him the picture of nonchalance at the plate. He seemed completely relaxed and comfortable, which he insists is the only recipe for a satisfactory stance. Joe doesn't say other batters should copy his stance but that no batter should employ a stance in which he feels uncomfortable. The very nature of DiMag's stance made him a late swinger. Some of Joe's best hits came, as the players phrase it, "right out of the catcher's glove."

One ball game DiMaggio invariably refers to when seized upon by a soul-searching interviewer is the All-Star game of 1936, played at Braves Field. That was DiMag's freshman year and he says he entered the game with a feeling that the world, or at least, the American League, was his oyster. Joe still thinks that that game, in which he played an uncertain outfield, went hitless, popped up and hit into a double play, was the poorest he ever played, considering its importance.

"I was just over-confident," he declares. "It was the first setback I had ever received in baseball, barring injuries, of course. On the ball field everything had run smoothly in my three years on the Pacific Coast League and there was no appreciable difference during my half-season in the American League. I was going great and it looked as though the game had been invented for my special benefit.

"When that 1936 All-Star game was over, I was the saddest, bluest guy you ever saw in the clubhouse. I'd been up five times without getting the ball out of the infield, had gummed up two balls in the outfield and left several runners stranded. The papers did a pretty good job on me, which I deserved. This was my first national game, so to speak, and I turned out to be a Grade A bust."

Joe McCarthy, who managed the Yankees during DiMaggio's first eight seasons, was the American League All-Star manager that afternoon and he stopped by DiMag's locker for a brief moment. "Don't let it get you down, kid," said McCarthy. Just that and no more.

DiMaggio didn't let the incident get him down but he never let himself forget it, either. He learned an invaluable lesson that day, the lesson being that nothing comes easily. For all of his seeming nonchalance at the plate, his facility in hauling down drives in the outfield, DiMag never ceased to bear down. He made it look easy but he never took it easily.

No better proof of what the public expected of the Clipper can be offered than the fact that writers frequently referred to 1946 as Joe's "bad year." It was the only time in his first eleven years with the Yankees that he failed to hit .300, failed by a matter of seven base hits. He batted .290, knocked in 95 runs and hit 25 home runs. And that was in his first season back after three years in service, a season in which he was beset by personal troubles, as an attempted reconciliation with his wife failed, and harassed by a tangled financial status. It was DiMag's "bad year," all right, but 80 per cent of the players in the majors today would settle for one like it at the plate.

Joe's personal life has been as tangled as his ball playing has been smooth. His marriage went on the rocks when he enlisted, although it had been embarked on a stormy sea before the crash. Mrs. DiMaggio retained custody of Little Joe and the father is able to see him only on week ends. The separation has made the relationship between father and son closer than ever, for when the Clipper was in New York, which was eight or ten months a year, Little Joe was all the family he had.

Business never could get DiMaggio's concentration and he embarked on many a deal which hurt him financially. It wasn't until after the 1947 season, when Joe came into the top salary brackets, that he had his snarled business affairs assume a semblance of order. Since then he has done very well and was able to leave baseball, or at least, the playing phase of it, with a worth-while nest egg.

For a person who came from humble beginnings, DiMaggio had a strange disregard for a dollar. He wasn't a coal-oil Johnny but he always acted as though there were plenty more where it came from. It was after the 1947 World Series that DiMag got his first big contractual raise. It was then, at thirty-three, that he realized nobody could go on forever and then that he developed a consciousness of the need for security.

Joe was born in Martinez, California, on November 25, 1914, the eighth of nine children. His father, a Sicilian immigrant, moved hs brood to San Francisco shortly after Joe was born and before the arrival of the ninth DiMaggio, Dominic.

The DiMaggio income stemmed from the fishing ventures of Papa DiMaggio and the older brothers and was precarious, to put it mildly. The Clipper looks back on those days without self-consciousness.

"We weren't poor in the sense that we were ever cold or hungry," he says, "but there never was any extra money in the house for luxuries. I can remember having to miss two movies which I wanted very much to see, Al Jolson's first talking picture, *The Jazz Singer*, and a war picture, *All Quiet on the Western Front*. I think they were charging two-bits in the movie houses in my neighborhood at that time but they might as well have been charging ten dollars. And I can remember walking two miles, or maybe more, to play ball and then walking back after the game was over. Even carfare was in the luxury class when I was a kid. You know how it was in those days."

The queasy stomach which was to plague DiMaggio with ulcers when he was an adult was present even when he was a kid. He couldn't help out on the family fishing expeditions because the roll of the small boat and the odor of the fish made him ill. His part of the family chores was to clean and repair the boat and the fishing nets.

Joe, as well as all of his brothers, sought extra work to augment the family income. Restless, DiMaggio bounced around as an errand boy, odd-job "man" and the other run of the mill tasks by which boys acquire pocket money. With the DiMaggios, however, it wasn't pocket money, it was table money. Every cent he earned was turned over to the household. Joe recalled that his most lucrative job was selling newspapers, at which he sometimes made as much as a dollar a day. "Counting tips, of course," he added seriously.

While DiMaggio was in his hotel suite in Manhattan relating these boyhood experiences, a bellhop knocked on the door to return Joe's automatic record player and to tell him that Miss Tallulah Bankhead, a guest at the same hotel, sent her thanks for its use. It was an incongruity that pointed up the rags-to-riches rise attained by DiMaggio through the medium of baseball.

On a balmy afternoon in March, 1949, DiMaggio, Phil Rizzuto and Yogi Berra were sipping beers at Egan's Grill on St. Petersburg Beach. Practice was over and throughout baseball a bottle of beer after a workout, or a game, is regarded as relaxing. Only DiMaggio didn't seem in the least relaxed. Rizzuto and Berra left to shoot a game of pool next door and a reporter asked Joe what made him so moody.

"That thing is growing back again," he said. "I can feel it every time I try to run hard. Maybe I'm through."

DiMag said more than that but that was the gist of it. Joe had played through most of the 1948 season with an excruciating pain in his right heel as the result of a calcium deposit known as a bone spur. He had been operated on for it in November, leaving the hospital in Baltimore on Thanksgiving Eve. Until after the New Year, he was practically a hermit in his hotel room, getting around on crutches. When the cast was removed and the crutches discarded, Joe was able to walk without pain and there was no reason to believe that the operation had not been 100 per cent successful.

When spring training opened March 1, at St. Petersburg, DiMaggio discovered he couldn't run without feeling that pain in his heel which had existed the year before. He flew back to Johns Hopkins immediately for X rays and was told that the spur was not growing back, as he feared. He returned to St. Pete but the evidence of the X rays and the opinions of the doctors did not convince the Clipper that the spur was not there. The same pain was there and that seemed more convincing to Joe than any amount of medical explanations.

It was after his return to St. Petersburg that he had the foregoing conversation at Egan's, the first time he ever voiced the fear that he might be through. That fear was to remain with DiMaggio for the rest of spring training and for nearly half of the American League season. Indeed, before the barnstorming tour on the way home was completed, Joe had again left the club, flying from Dallas, Texas, where he had to quit after two innings of exhibition play, to Baltimore for further treatments.

Casey Stengel, back from the minors to manage in the majors for the third time, handled DiMaggio with great understanding. Throughout the training period he allowed DiMag to judge when he should play and when he should not. When the regular season opened and it was apparent that DiMaggio was a cripple of uncertain status, Joe went into a blue funk. He secluded himself in his hotel room and saw nobody, save Toots Shor, the restaurateur, and George Solotaire, manager of a ticket agency, both of whom have been his close friends for years.

Alone in his hotel room, DiMaggio brooded about being

hrough. He began to wonder about his eyes going back on
him, as well as his legs. He could get no satisfaction from doc-
ors, for only rest could be prescribed. And Joe couldn't even
est, for he tossed wide awake half the night, ridden by night-
mares in which he faced a future without baseball.

The miracle happened without advance signs. One morning his heel pained him when he put his foot upon the floor
or the first time and the next morning it didn't pain him. He
reported at Yankee Stadium, took batting practice until his
palms were blistered.

Slowly he began to spend more time at the plate and
finally took an outfield workout.

When Joe felt that he was ready, he told Manager Stengel
he would like to play a few innings in a night exhibition game
against the Giants. Casey told him to go as far as he liked and
Joe, to his own surprise as much as that of anybody else, went
the full nine innings. It was characteristic of DiMaggio, perhaps the greatest ball player of his time, that he chose to give
himself his big test in an exhibition game. The Yankees were
surprisingly leading the league and Joe didn't want to do anything to handicap them!

After the exhibition the Yanks moved on to Boston, to
meet the Red Sox, their strongest rivals and a team, as it
turned out, they were to beat for the pennant in the final game
of the year. DiMaggio got a single on his first time at bat
against Maurice McDermott, after having missed the first 66
games the Yankees played that year. Later in the game Joe
blasted a home run over the left field fence and sent the Yankee
bench into ecstasies. In the next game of the series Joe hit two
more home runs and in the third game he hit his fourth!

It was the most spectacular comeback in baseball history.

DiMaggio became the most talked of person in baseball, maybe in America for the next few weeks. *Life* made him its cover boy, devoted six pages to his comeback and purportedly paid him $6,000 to put his by-line over the story.

Once back in the lineup, DiMag never let up. He was the outstanding player in the All-Star game at Ebbets Field with a double and single which drove in three runs and, proportionately, from his return in late June until he was stricken with virus pneumonia in mid-September, Joe's work matched that of any of his early years.

Two weeks before the end of the season, when the Red Sox began inching uncomfortably close to the Yankees, DiMaggio ran a fever and had to take to his bed. His ailment was diagnosed as virus pneumonia but there were rumors that he was a polio victim, so great is the power of exaggeration. And so mighty was the legend of the Clipper's hard luck.

With DiMaggio again in sick bay, the Red Sox caught and passed the Yankees in the last week of the season. Joe McCarthy's team came into Yankee Stadium on a Saturday, the penultimate day of the season, holding a one-game lead. The pennant was theirs if they could split the two remaining games.

It so happened that this Saturday had been designated as "Joe DiMaggio Day," a day conceived before he fell before the onslaughts of the virus. Weak, gaunt and haggard, 15 pounds underweight, Joe stood at home plate with his mother, his brothers and Little Joe by his side. He received gifts which ranged from a speedboat to an oil painting, from rosary beads to a gold belt buckle. And, of course, the customary automobile. Mayor William V. O'Dwyer and other civic dignitaries advanced on the public address system and told Joe how good he was. And then the game started and Joe went out and proved it!

Too weak to pull the ball, DiMag dropped a couple of hits into right field and the Yanks went on to win and tie up the pennant race. And, on Sunday, again with Joe hitting to right field instead of left, they beat the Red Sox again and won the pennant.

On the momentum of those two games with the Red Sox, the Yankees stormed through the World Series to defeat the Dodgers in five games. And, in the fifth game, played in Brooklyn, DiMaggio whaled a home run into the upper deck at Ebbets Field. The game, and the Series was over by then but the crowd stood as one man to give the Clipper an ovation as he trotted around the bases. Joe had come a long way since that March afternoon in Egan's Grill when he voiced the fear that he was through.

For the first time in his career, major or minor, Joe was benched in 1950. For the first two thirds of the season, the Jolter couldn't seem to untrack himself. He batted around .275 and the talk was that he was washed up, despite certain concrete evidence to the contrary. He was hitting the ball with his old power—when he was hitting it. His homer total and his runs-batted-in mark were running ahead of his batting average.

As the American League race waxed hotter and injuries seemed to have doomed the Yanks, Casey Stengel made a daring move. He decided to rest Joe for the home stretch run. It was the first time the Clipper was out of the lineup for any reason other than injuries. The brief respite paid terrific dividends. With Joe in the van, the Yanks came roaring down to the wire to eliminate Detroit, Cleveland and the rejuvenated Red Sox. DiMaggio hit over .400 in this stretch, regained a seasonal rating of .300 and was a key-man as the Yankees swept the Philadelphia Whiz Kids right out of the World Series in four straight.

It was DiMaggio's ninth Series—out of twelve active seasons, a record unparalleled in baseball. He won the second game in Philadelphia with a home run into Shibe Park's upper deck in the tenth, after popping up four times and made a terrific back-handed stop of Granny Hamner's double to prevent a possible homer in the third, saving that game. He doubled on his first time at bat in the final game to knock out Bob Miller and start the Phils on their way out of the Series.

About the only period in DiMaggio's life when baseball wasn't the alpha and omega of his existence was when he was twelve years old and, inflamed by the exploits of two fellow San Franciscans, Maurice McLaughlin and Bill Johnston, he decided to become a tennis player. Within a year or two, Joe had forgotten about tennis and was firmly set on a baseball career. His older brother, Vince, was playing week-end ball and getting a couple of bucks for it and Joe decided that sandlot baseball would be the ideal medium through which to increase the family's bankroll.

Spike Hennessey, a scout for the San Francisco Seals, invited DiMaggio to work out with the club at the tag end of the 1932 season. Vince already had been recalled from a farm club where the Seals had him under contract. Augie Galan, the club's regular shortstop, received permission to leave for a Honolulu vacation before the season ended and Vince told

Ike Caveney, the Seals' manager, that his kid brother Joe could fill in. Joe did just that and hit a triple off Ted Pillette, a former major leaguer, on his first time at bat in organized ball.

What DiMaggio showed at short in those few games was good enough for the Seals to bring him to training camp in 1933 and sign him to a contract, calling for $225 a month, before the season opened. Although listed as a shortstop, Joe got his first chance in the outfield and he's been there ever since.

All DiMaggio had at eighteen was a natural ability to hit a baseball. The niceties of the game were to be acquired later. "I was really pea-green," confessed Joe looking back through the years. "I remember a reporter asking me for a 'quote' on something or other and I was so dumb I didn't even know what a 'quote' was. I thought it was some kind of soft drink."

DiMag wasn't pea-green up at the plate, however. In his freshman year, 1933, he batted safely in 61 consecutive games in the Coast League, breaking a record set by Jack Ness for 49 games, nearly twenty years before. The streak by the rookie turned the spotlight on Joe and he hasn't escaped its glare since. Major league scouts swarmed around San Francisco like locusts.

Charley Graham, the San Francisco owner, was one of baseball's pioneers. He had sold ball players to the majors before, and was to keep selling them until his death many years later. He stood off the bids, reasoning that Joe was a natural and that another season with the Seals would help the club in the race, and at the gate, and would put a higher value on DiMaggio.

The 1934 season had scarcely opened when the now notorious DiMaggio jinx struck for the first time. Stepping out of an automobile, in which he had been riding in a cramped position, Joe felt his left knee pop on him. He tried to dismiss it to Manager Caveney as a Charley horse but it was obviously more serious. Eventually, DiMag had to spend six weeks in a splint.

Bill Essick and Joe Devine, the Yankee scouts for Pacific Coast territory, saw that DiMaggio was favoring his knee for the balance of the season but refused to believe he was washed up. Essick told Graham that if a San Francisco physician, a Dr. Spencer, were given permission to examine and treat DiMaggio, the Yankees would be willing to give $25,000 and four players for Joe and allow Graham his services for 1935.

Dr. Spencer's treatments were efficacious and the Yanks completed the deal after the close of the 1934 season, Joe being purchased for delivery in the spring of 1936. That the Yankees acted when they did was a fortuitous break for their exchequer, for all DiMag did in his final season in the Coast League was bat .398, making 270 base hits, of which 34 were home runs. By that time, San Francisco could have got as much as $100,000 for DiMaggio but he was Yankee property.

Horace Stoneham, president of the Giants, Carl Hubbell, director of the Giant farm system and a couple of sports writers were sitting in a New York restaurant shortly after the Yankees had out-wrestled the Dodgers in the ding-dong, seven-game World Series of 1947. They talked of this and of that, of the startling suddenness with which Larry MacPhail had quit baseball, of the great catch little Al Gionfriddo had made against DiMaggio, of the dramatic two-bagger by Cookie Lavagetto which robbed Floyd Bevens not only of a no-hitter but of victory. Mostly, though, they talked of the Yankee Clipper.

"Yessir," drawled Hubbell, "that DiMaggio—he's a pro."

And with that Hubbell summed it all up. DiMaggio's

greatest accolade comes from his fellow professionals. His great skills were apparent to the fans in the stands but only those who have been through the mill themselves can properly appreciate the superlative style with which DiMag brought these skills into play.

Few ball players have enjoyed the artistic esteem in which DiMaggio was held by his contemporaries. Those who played with Joe, or against him, knew that they were looking at one of the all-time greats.

In 1941, when DiMaggio made American League history by hitting in 56 consecutive games, he was in danger of having his streak halted by the Browns, after he had hit in 36 straight games. Bob Muncrief had stopped him three times but on the fourth try, Joe cracked him for a single.

Since the Yankees were well ahead at the time, DiMaggio's hit meant nothing except to his streak and there was some discussion afterward as to why Muncrief didn't walk the Clipper.

"I couldn't have done that," said Bob. "It wouldn't have been fair to him or to me. He's the greatest player I've ever seen."

That Muncrief was not alone in this viewpoint was demonstrated two days later, in the third game of the Brownie series. Again Joe was held hitless coming up to the ninth and this time there were three Yankees slated to hit before he did. The leadoff hitter singled and the next batter sacrificed to avoid the double play contingency and assure DiMag of coming to bat. With two out, a man on second and first base open, the dictates of strategy are to walk the batter. Manager Luke Sewell ordered Eldon Auker to pitch to Joe and the Clipper smacked out a two-bagger.

When Joe was sidelined in the spring of 1949, Manager Stengel adopted a you're-the-boss attitude toward him. He told DiMag that whenever he felt ready to play, he'd use him and that Joe could bench himself at any time he felt his injuries bothering him.

The temptation to use DiMaggio, crippled heel and all, as a pinch-hitter must have been strong. The Yankees had one key player injured after another and Stengel must have felt that there were times when a pinch-hit by DiMaggio would have worked wonders but he refrained. Asked about it, Casey replied in a manner that showed he, too, was not lacking in big league class.

"Why use the fellow on one leg?" said Stengel impatiently. "When he's ready, he'll let me know. He's been too great a ball player to be wasted or made a fool of." Casey ended his sentence on a preposition but on a sound proposition.

DiMaggio was essentially a team-man, for all of his undeniable individual skills. Some years ago, vacationing in Florida, a lady, or rather, a woman fan ran across Joe and started to berate him about the final game of the 1941 World Series in which he and Whit Wyatt, the Dodger pitcher, had exchanged heated words and almost came to blows.

"Wyatt made you look like a bum that day," she shrieked.

"I guess he did at that," agreed Joe amiably enough, "but you forget one thing. I wasn't playing Wyatt. The Yankees were playing the Dodgers and the Yankees won."

For the second time in his life, DiMaggio saw the Yankees win a fourth straight pennant in 1952, but this time Joe was on the outside looking in. To be specific, he was conducting television shows before and after the home games in the Stadium and not too happy about it.

It came as no shock when DiMaggio failed to return to his television show in 1953. He gave the impression that he felt it was a poor substitute for playing the game itself. Joe had guests on his show before and after the games but he never really opened them up with prying questions. As time went on, he achieved a certain relaxed air but he rarely brought to the show his own vast knowledge of the game, nor did he attempt to exploit that of the ball players whom he had as his guests.

Rarely has there been such a complete drop-out of a top notch performer in sports. Although TV fans saw the Clipper before and after all home games, and on his Sunday morning filmed shows, few saw him in person. He disappeared from his usual haunts and missed no opportunities to fly back to his native California.

The only time Joe's name appeared in the newspapers was when the gossip columns linked his name with the curvaceous Miss Marilyn Monroe, a movie performer. And even that eventually died out.

When Dom DiMaggio announced early in the 1953 season that he was retiring from the Red Sox outfield, the name of DiMaggio slipped out of major league box scores entirely, for the first time—barring the war years—since Joe came to the Yankees in 1936. It is baseball's loss.

CHAPTER IV

THE SPRINGFIELD RIFLE
(Vic Raschi)

BY TOM MEANY

It was, by and large, an unusual spring trip that the Yankees indulged in in 1947. They were flown from La-Guardia Field to San Juan, Puerto Rico, where they played a series of games against local teams under the sponsorship of the Don-Q Rum Company at a ball field named after a bantamweight boxing champion Sixto Escobar Parque. Without drawing a deep breath, they were flown from San Juan to La Guaira, Venezuela, and driven up the side of a mountain to Caracas, where they played in a park named after a brewery and under the sponsorship of a private citizen, Senor Alberto Winkleman.

After sampling a couple of local clubs, the Yankees engaged in a series with the Dodgers at Caracas and then took to the airways once again, this time flying to Havana for another series with Brooklyn. This latter series led to a rhubarb which eventually caused Commissioner Chandler, for reasons known only to himself, to suspend Leo Durocher, the Brooklyn manager, for the entire season.

When the Yankees finally flew from Cuba to their home base at St. Petersburg, Florida, some of the air-weary travelers felt as tired as the octogenarians who inhabit that city's green benches. It was little wonder that a great many people were up in the air at the conclusion of so lengthy a trip. Larry MacPhail, the Yankee impressario, was high on a rookie pitcher, one Don Johnson, a right hander, twenty years old and lately returned from service, who had seen limited action with Kansas City and Newark in 1944.

Johnson was a picture pitcher. He looked like the answer to a manager's prayer and watching him in the early drills Manager Bucky Harris absorbed some of MacPhail's enthusiasm. There was another right handed rookie on the staff, Vic Raschi, who had come up from Newark at the tag end of the 1946 season to win a couple of games for the Yanks but Vic was lost in the general hoop-la over Johnson.

Although some voiced the opinion that Johnson might profit from another year in the minors, MacPhail insisted he was ready right now. Thus when the time came to pare down the squad, Raschi was sent to Portland in the Pacific Coast League, which probably gave him the mileage record for 1947.

A few starts convinced Harris that Johnson wasn't going to be any help that season. It was also apparent to Bucky that the Yankees, with a little boost in the pitching department, could win the 1947 pennant. Spud Chandler, ace of the pre-war years, wasn't up to it but Allie Reynolds, obtained from the Indians, was pitching great ball and so was Frank Shea, a freshman. And Joe Page was blossoming forth as a relief pitcher.

MacPhail's worst enemies never accused him of not being

an opportunist. Larry got Harris the help he needed, picking up the fabulous Bobo Newsom on waivers from Washington on July 11 and exercising the option on Raschi to bring Vic back from Portland. Both joined the club in Chicago at a time when the Yanks were in the midst of a winning streak which was eventually to tie a 41-year-old American League record before it stopped at nineteen.

On a hot, humid Sunday, the two new pitching acquisitions were turned loose against the White Sox at Comiskey Park. Newsom celebrated his fourteenth job with a major league club by winning and Raschi, showing none of the effects of his long travels, won also. The Yankee streak was kept going and Raschi was on his way to his first steady job in baseball.

Travel really wasn't anything new for Raschi. The season before, his first year out of service, Vic had pitched for Binghamton in the Eastern League, Newark in the International and the Yankees in the American. Oddly enough, in 1947 Vic was sent to Portland when the club was playing in Cleveland and came back when the team was in Chicago. Raschi had won eight games and lost two for Jim Turner at Portland and his Yankee record for the balance of 1947 was 7-2, indicating the big right hander was taking his travels in stride.

The late Gene McCann, celebrated Yankee scout, wore a white tie with every costume for reasons known only to himself. He picked up many a star for the Yanks in his long career and Raschi is probably the last. Gene spotted Vic when he was pitching high school ball in his native Springfield, Massachusetts, and convinced the boy that he could serve his future best by signing with the Yanks.

There was no bird-dog, as baseball terms an auxiliary

scout, to flush out Raschi for McCann. Gene had served the Yanks as a baseball executive in Springfield when the Bombers had a farm club there and he made it his business to prowl the high school fields and the sandlots in search of talent.

Raschi was willing to play ball and to be paid for it, but he first wanted to complete his education. That was all right with McCann, who had what the trade calls "connections" and he told the big Italian kid that he was enrolling him at Manhattan College, hard by Spuyten Duyvil, the stream which connects the Harlem with the Hudson. The prospect pleased Vic, but when he climbed the hill to Manhattan in September he discovered there was no record of his registration. A hasty phone call to the Yankee office followed and eventually Raschi found himself on the campus of the College of William and Mary in Williamsburg, Virginia. Today Vic holds a Bachelor of Science degree from William and Mary, so he scarcely comes under the "tramp athlete" heading.

Raschi is grateful to William and Mary for more than an education, for it was there that he met his future wife, Sally Glen, of Rochester, New York. The Raschis have adopted a French war orphan and, although they have never seen the child, they are paying for its rehabilitation and upkeep. They also have two children of their own.

At Springfield Tech High, under Coach Irvin (Chief) Walmer, Raschi was an outstanding end in football and star basketball player as well as a member of the baseball nine. Norman Miller, a sports writer for the United Press in New York, was with Vic at Springfield Tech and remembers him as playing the outfield.

"We used to play our ball games at Blunt Park and the outfield was always ringed with parked autos," recalls Miller.

"I remember Vic in the outfield one afternoon shagging flies. A long one was hit and Raschi set out after it and didn't stop until he had put his head right through the windshield of one of the parked cars. He still carries the scars. The next time I saw Vic he was on the pitching mound. It may have been the collision with the windshield which caused him to change his baseball position."

Raschi was already prominent as a pitcher when McCann first spotted him. As a matter of fact, Vic's first view of Yankee Stadium came as a result of his pitching prowess. The sandlot team for which he was pitching, the Ruth Elizabeth Trojans, won the city championship and its members were rewarded with a trip to the Bronx ball park. Little did Vic dream that some dozen years later nearly 8,000 fans would journey from Springfield to see him pitch in that same ball park. On the books of the New York, New Haven & Hartford, the excursion from Springfield to New York in September 1948 is the largest single rail movement of civilians in transportation history.

The Raschi family doubtless looks with mixed emotions on baseball for while it provided one brother, Vic, with gold and glory, it deprived a younger brother, Eugene, of his eyesight. Eugene twice was struck with batted balls, once when he was a child of nine and again when he was sixteen, and lost his vision as a result. Yet there is no more ardent Yankee fan in the country than Eugene, who follows all the games by radio and when he attends games in either Boston or New York, follows them carefully through the assistance of a companion. He also keeps elaborate statistics on the pitching progress of brother Vic.

Raschi's first assignment as Yankee property was at Amsterdam, New York, in the Canadian-American League, where he had a 10-6 record. He was advanced to Norfolk in the Piedmont League the next year but had a poor season, winning only four games while losing ten. Then came three years in the air corps. He was promoted, in 1946, to Binghamton in the Eastern League, where he split 20 decisions before getting another boost, this to Newark, where he won one game out of three. And he finally finished out the season by winning a couple of games for the Yankees, as related.

A big, strapping fellow Raschi always had a live fast ball and is always high up in the strikeout totals. He has the sweeping curve to go with it and finally added the inevitable extra pitch, the popular slider. "I can pitch a slider without effort," explained Vic, "and decided to develop that pitch rather than a knuckler or something of that type because I knew I could throw the slider without injuring my arm."

There is no doubt that Raschi profited in his brief stay at Portland under Turner. Milkman Jim later was promoted to a coach's job with the Yankees and Manager Casey Stengel gives Turner complete control of his pitchers. Jim, who came to the Braves in 1937 at the age of 33 to lead the league in shutouts and earned runs and finish up as a 20-game winner, is an excellent handler of pitchers.

Turner, who deliberately avoids credit for the development of any pitchers who have come under his instruction, recalls Raschi's work at Portland with affection and still winces when he recalls the Yankees' decision to recall him from the Beavers.

"Because of the difference in time, I was still in bed when I got a phone call from George Weiss, the Yankee general manager," related Jim. "As soon as I heard his voice I knew exactly what was going to happen. George asked if I had received his wire, which I hadn't. He told me he was taking back Raschi, who had won eight and lost two. 'Don't be too upset, though,' he said, 'we'll send you a replacement.' I knew no matter who the Yanks sent it wouldn't be anybody as good as Vic. It turned out to be a right hander named Edson Bahr, who took thirteen days to arrive and won two and lost three for me."

The long trail which started when the eagle eye of White-Tie Gene McCann spotted Raschi as a high school kid in Springfield paid off when Vic defeated Jim Konstanty and the Philadelphia Whiz Kids by 1 to 0 in the opening game of the 1950 World Series at Shibe Park. Oddly enough, it was the third straight opening game of a Series which had been decided by a 1-0 score. Johnny Sain had scored similarly over Bob Feller for the Braves at Boston in 1948 and Allie Reynolds over Brooklyn's Don Newcombe at Yankee Stadium in 1949.

In many respects, Raschi's game was better than either of its predecessors. Sain allowed four singles and walked none in beating Cleveland and Reynolds allowed two hits, a single and double, and walked four while turning back the Dodgers. Vic allowed the Phils two singles and walked only one.

Because of the importance of a World Series opener, Raschi considers that the best game he ever has pitched and rightly so. He was in command from start to finish. Vic retired the first 13 Phils to face him before he permitted Puddin' Head Jones a single through the box with one out in the fifth. Granny Hamner flied out and then Andy Seminick singled to left, but Raschi fanned Mike Goliat to end the inning. Jones took second on Seminick's single, the only Whiz Kid to progress that far. Eddie Waitkus, who walked with one out in the sixth, was the only other Phillie to get on base and Raschi set down the last 11 in order.

Raschi is a fine competitor and has turned in some of his best pitching under stress. In 1950 on August 4, he beat Feller and the Indians 1 to 0 in Cleveland, allowing only three hits and walking two, while fanning eight. It kept the Yanks within two games of Detroit, the team they eventually were to beat out for the pennant.

The victory over Feller was the opening wedge to a distinction which is unique among pitchers. Although Raschi has never pitched a no-hitter, he has the record of retiring 32 batters in succession. Against Cleveland the day he beat Bobby, Vic retired the last 20 Indians to face him and in his next start, against the Red Sox at the Stadium, he got the first dozen batters in a row before a man reached first.

When the White Sox began sagging at the end of July, 1951, Raschi stopped them before 72,217 at Yankee Stadium in a game in which he fanned a dozen to take the major league lead in strikeouts. He had to quit this game with two out in the ninth when a line drive by Chico Carrasquel, Sox shortstop, smashed him on the pitching hand. Vic, by the way, had opened the 1951 season, bidding for his third straight season of 20 or more victories, with a 5-0 shutout of the slugging Red Sox.

Raschi entered the 1953 season without any club in the American League holding a bulge over him in games won and lost. His won and lost percentage was higher than that of any other active pitcher in the American League.

Raschi has been around long enough to know that it takes help to win ball games. He pitched an excellent game in the second game of the 1949 World Series but was beaten 1 to 0 by Preacher Roe of the Dodgers when Gil Hodges singled with two out in the second to score Jackie Robinson, who had opened the inning with a two-bagger. In the fifth game of that Series, Vic pitched rather spottily and needed help in the seventh when Hodges tagged him for a three-run homer. Joe Page was able to hold the Brooks the rest of the way and Vic had his first World Series victory by the somewhat sloppy score of 10 to 6.

Although Raschi won 21 games for the Yanks in 1951, he was bothered from time to time with a trick knee, an old injury which hampered his pitching. The knee was operated on after the season ended. He split two decisions in the Series against the Giants, emerging the winning pitcher in the sixth and final game, although he left in the seventh inning with the score 4 to 1 in his favor.

Although Raschi finished 1952 with his best percentage, .727, as a Yankee regular, he won only 16 games. He was credited with two of the four Yankee victories over the Dodgers in the World Series, one a three-hitter. He won the second and sixth games, each time evening the Series and wiping out a Dodger advantage. Periodically, he gave signs that he had not completely recovered from the operation that he had had on his knee.

Because of his three years in service, Raschi was 28 when he came back to the Yankees as a regular and, despite his undoubted stamina, the charmed circle of 200 victories seems beyond his reach. Nevertheless, his work since he has become a starter with the Yankees stamps him as one of the outstanding pitchers in baseball.

CHAPTER V

HEAP BIG CHIEF
(Allie Reynolds)

BY MILTON GROSS

Somehow word had gone out a full week before that Allie Reynolds, the Yankee pitcher, had rented the house for the baseball season and was bringing his family up from Oklahoma to live on that quiet, tree-lined street in Leonia, New Jersey.

Now the Reynolds family was in its temporary home and the neighbors were there to greet them—youngsters and adults, boys and girls. The street in front of the modest two-story building had become a hangout. The kids, autograph books clutched in their hands, waited for Allie to come and go.

Allie's nine-year-old son, J. D., became a courier, carrying blank pieces of paper in to his father, and inscribed pieces back to the kids. Thirteen-year-old Allie Dale didn't have to go far to find his way to a ball game. It was there in front of his house any time he wanted it. Even 12-year-old Bobby Kaye, Allie Dale's sister, was allowed to take part in the game, for the glamor of a big-league father had rubbed off on her.

A day or two after the Reynolds family had settled down,

a man came along with his son. He paced off the distance between an imaginary pitcher's mound and what should be home plate, spread a handkerchief on the pavement as a target, and proceeded to have the boy warm up. As the boy pitched, his Dad kept glancing toward the Reynolds' house. Finally, he walked up to it, rang the bell, and when Allie answered, asked him to come out and see if the boy had stuff.

When Reynolds said he would come out to look at the youngster pitching to his Dad, the man hastened down the path so quickly he lost his footing and fell, ripping his pants and skinning his knee. He jumped up with a laugh, ran back to the improvised home plate, and shouted, "C'mon, boy, burn 'em in! We got a real pitcher to umpire. Let's show him what you can do!"

"I wonder," said Allie later that night, "what kind of pitcher I would be today if I'd had that same kind of encouragement when I was a kid out in Bethany, Oklahoma."

The impression seems to be that Allie, with or without encouragement in his youth, surely has become an outstanding pitcher.

Although the Yankees traded Joe Gordon for Allie following the 1946 season, Reynolds' reputation hadn't been too solid at Cleveland. Through 1949, Allie still hadn't developed a substantial foundation despite the 52 victories with which he had been credited in the three years since the trade. In 1949, Allie was credited with 17 victories, while being charged with only six defeats. But most of the season he rode aboard relief pitcher Joe Page's back, hurling only four complete games, so that newspaper editors with an eye toward a gag almost invariably listed the Yankees' winning pitcher as "Reynolds-Page."

Allie had developed a reputation for timidity on the hill.

Rightly or wrongly, he had been labeled a tabby cat pitcher who didn't like the tight ball games. His critics pointed to his 10-3 pitching victory in the 1947 Series as the kind of game in which Reynolds reveled. No pressure, no heat, plenty of breathing space.

It wasn't that way in the opening 1949 World Series game. There was heat, humidity, constant pressure. There were 66,224 spectators. And there was Reynolds besting Don Newcombe and holding the Dodgers to two hits as the Yankees broke from the Series barrier with a 1-0 victory on Tommy Henrich's homer in the ninth. Three games later, Allie loosed the tie that bound him as he reversed the roles and helped Ed Lopat to a Series win by hurling three perfect innings of relief ball after slamming the door shut in the face of a Brooklyn rally.

"I stood on the top of the dugout steps and watched the ball going into the stands to win that first game for me," Allie recalls, "and I couldn't believe that it was happening. Ever since I was a kid, I'd had the overpowering feeling that the breaks would never be mine. It was the first time I had come up with the right game in the right place."

Can one game in a lifetime of games change a man? Allie thinks that one altered his outlook. His wife, Earlene, whom Allie married when he was only 18 and a sophomore in college, and she was 16, agrees wholeheartedly.

"I don't know how I can explain it to you without making it sound silly," she says. "The best example I can think of is this. Last Winter, I asked Allie to come out and take rhumba and samba lessons, and he went gladly. He got to like it and we started going out dancing regularly. He never cared for evenings out before.

77

"There aren't many people who understand Allie the way I do. He's a strange man. His face rarely shows what he's thinking. He's lived inside himself mostly, but now he's begun to live outside as well. To understand it, you must know his background and appreciate how it was when he was a child and how difficult it was for him when we married.

"My goodness," said Mrs. Reynolds. "Allie Dale is only 15. When I think that I was only one year older than he when I married his father, I wonder how we made it. We had to be grownups while we were still children. We weren't ready for it. And Allie wasn't ready to be a big-league pitcher when he became one."

As is so often the case, it is not the man but his mate who supplies the key to the puzzle. Here lies the answer to Reynolds' strange record and the raps he has taken while laboring in baseball's vineyards. The most surprising feature is that Allie ever managed to become a big-leaguer at all, much less a pitcher who can command $40,000 from the Yankees, which is what he was paid this season. He didn't start in organized baseball until he was 22, and only a fractured vertebra, an old football injury, which had kept him out of the war, paradoxically resulted in his promotion to the Indians. At 25, he was a big-leaguer, but in name and uniform only, and it was harder on this father of three children to learn when every pitch meant so much at home. A man works better when he's loose and unencumbered than when there are many strings attached, despite the copybook maxims to the contrary.

We go back to sun-drenched, deeply religious Bethany, where Allie was born on February 10, 1917. His parents, like most of their neighbors in this little community 12 miles outside of Stillwater, Oklahoma, were members of the Nazarene

Church. To this day, the Nazarene influence in Bethany is strong. Cigarettes and beer cannot be sold there. Movies are frowned upon. Dress and custom are severe.

The college basketball team, for instance, still wears full-length sweat pants for games rather than the bare-kneed shorts that are commonplace elsewhere. The community prefers to keep bare skin hidden from public view. Not so long ago, the players also had to wear long-sleeved sweat shirts over their bare-armed jerseys while performing. Track meets still are held outside of town at some teachers' college, and under county rather than town auspices, because sprinters and such can then strip down as trackmen do at all other places.

If restrictions were rigid for the Reynolds neighbors, they were especially strict for Allie, whose father felt so devoutly about his religion that after his son was born he matriculated at the Nazarene seminary at Pasadena, California, where he studied to become a minister.

Reverend D. C. Reynolds, who lived most of his life in Indian territory and now is a traveling Nazarene evangelist, is half Creek Indian. Allie is therefore one-quarter Creek. While the Eastern mind conjures a vision of an Indian child running about a reservation wearing little more than a loin cloth, Allie's childhood doesn't fit any such picture.

Until he entered his senior year at high school, Allie had never seen a football game. Until his junior year in college, he had never played on an organized baseball team. While he was courting his bride-to-be, the young lovers were unable to attend a picture show unless they defied the restrictions laid down by Allie's parents.

Even after Allie had demonstrated to his folks that their devout life was not for him, and they reluctantly agreed to allow him to go his way in sports and romance, the past occasionally reached forward and grabbed for him.

Secure in his newly found confidence, Allie can look back now and laugh at the aftermath of a college game he lost because of bases on balls when he was pitching for Oklahoma A. and M. The headline in the Stillwater paper the following day read, "Wildness Costs Reynolds Game."

As though defeat at the bats of Oklahoma, the Aggies' foremost rival, wasn't bad enough, Allie had to face the wrath of his 78-year-old grandmother when he got home.

As she read the headline, Allie's grandmother had exclaimed to Allie's father, "I warned you this would happen. That boy is going to the dogs."

At the risk of aggravating his still spry grandparent, Allie points out that the road he took as an athlete hardly has consigned him to perdition. "There was nothing I wanted to do more than take part in sports," Reynolds says. "But every time I tried, we'd have a new crisis in the family. Finally, after I was about to enter my senior year in high school, my father was assigned to a new parish at Capitol Hill, a suburb of Oklahoma City. I got him to agree that I could transfer there for school before he actually took over his new assignment, and then I made my stand. I insisted I wanted to go out for football. I was only 145 pounds then, but I threw my weight around. I threatened to leave home if I wasn't allowed to try, and Dad finally gave in.

"As I look back at it now, I'm sorry I ever played football, except that it was my springboard to baseball. But it took me three years to lose the muscular tightness I developed on the gridiron to get loosened up after I started in baseball.

"That didn't help either," Allie recalls, "and when you

add those years to the many years I'd have had in sports if I had been allowed to play like any other kid, I might have reached a peak much earlier. After all, I didn't begin to pitch until my junior year at A. and M.

"I was afraid that this late start would work against me. To show you how uncertain I was when the Indians signed me to a Springfield contract in 1939, I lied about my age. I cut off a couple of years, claiming I had been born in 1919. That's the age which still is erroneously listed for me in many record books to this day," Allie disclosed.

"I'm still not a real pitcher," he said, "all because of that late start. Maybe I'm just getting there. I mean, you've got to distinguish between a pitcher and a thrower. I was a thrower until that Series game in 1949. I never appreciated the advantage of being ahead of the batter. I must admit I'm still learning fundamentals, just getting the hang of inside baseball."

Fortunately for Allie, what he lacked in experience and early encouragement, he made up for in abundant natural talent. When Allie still was a student at Stillwater, the late Ed Gallagher, coach of the national championship Aggie wrestling team, besieged Reynolds with requests to become a grappler.

"He'd be a champion in no time," Gallagher said, "because he's the greatest natural athlete I've ever seen."

Gallagher wasn't just throwing compliments around. In no time at all, in his senior year in high school and freshman year in college, Allie established a fabulous reputation. When he tried out for Capitol Hill's championship football team, Allie had never played the game before, but he won a letter. On the basis of one season's performance in track, he was granted a scholarship to A. and M.

Allie ran the 100 in 9.8, tossed the javelin, and insists

to this day that had he concentrated on the 220 he could have approached world-record time. A season of track somehow added 20 pounds to the Reynolds frame and prompted Allie to report for football practice in his sophomore year. He made the team first crack, being used as a fullback out of a single wing because he was able to run well and block well.

One season of Spring football practice was enough for Allie. He took to spending his time around the baseball diamond. One afternoon he found himself standing beside Hank Iba, the baseball coach, at the batting cage while practice was on. In fraternity baseball, Allie had been averaging 14 strikeouts a game as a pitcher. Reynolds, under such circumstances, was no secret on the campus.

"How'd you like to try pitching some batting practice?" Iba asked Allie.

"Why not?" Reynolds answered.

"Get a glove and warm up a while," the coach suggested.

"Warm up? What for? I don't have to.

"If I ever did now what I did then, the hitters would throw their bats at me," Allie says. "But I wasn't going to allow any of those batters to hit me if I could help it. I threw to four men. Not a one of them got a foul off me."

As Allie recalls the story, Iba walked out to the mound at that point and asked Reynolds, "How much baseball have you played? You throw pretty hard."

"None," Reynolds answered, "except for fraternity games."

"I guess you better get a suit anyway," the coach replied.

Reynolds has two brothers, 32-year-old Brenton, and 30-year-old James. Allie broke Brenton's leg in a wrestling match when they were kids and eliminated him from any future sports competition. But with the breach in parental discipline that Allie had begun, Jim went on to become another football great at A. and M.

At present, Jim coaches football and track at Putnam City, Oklahoma, High School, and has decided to give up pro football. Unlike Allie, who received a bid from the New York Giants of the National League, but decided to spurn it for a pro baseball career, Jim played on the pro gridiron until 1949 when he was an All-Star American League right-halfback with the Richmond Rebels.

Before he lost his speed, Jim played with the Chicago Cardinals, Pittsburgh Steelers, and Green Bay Packers.

During the Yankees' first Western trip in 1951, Yogi Berra invited several of his teammates to a *bocce* ball game in his native St. Louis. Reynolds had never seen or heard of this peculiarly Italian lawn bowling game, but asked if he could come along.

"Do you think you can play it?" asked Tommy Henrich, who eventually teamed up with Allie against Berra and Phil Rizzuto.

"There isn't any game I can't play well," Allie answered in his usual poker-faced way.

Henrich laughs every time he remembers Allie's statement. With any other man, Tommy might have discounted it as an idle boast. With Allie, you can never be sure. He took up golf five years ago and already shoots in the high 70's. Pros have told him that if he played regularly, he could compete with fair chance of success in professional circles.

In college, Reynolds never went out for tennis regularly, but he made it a practice to take on the varsity members, and could beat them consistently. He even tried his hand at girls' field hockey one time when he thought that would help him keep in shape. For his ambition and pains, he received a cut head and a wife. The girl whose stick split Allie's skull was the one he decided to marry—and did.

Mrs. Reynolds is as adept at athletics as her husband. In high school, she won an award as the best all-around girl athlete. In self defense, she says, she took up golf three years ago, and already has reached the stage where she plays in the 80's. In 1949 she was beaten in an Oklahoma City women's tournament by the runner-up, 1-up, on the 18th hole.

Even Bobby Kaye is showing an inclination and decided talent in sports. She made her track team at Sequoyah School in Oklahoma City. One day she brought home an especially attractive school report. Allie examined the report card and said, "I guess you're about the smartest girl in the room."

"I really am not, Daddy," Bobby Kaye answered. "But I can run faster than any of them!"

The Reynolds family is a tightly knit unit, possibly because until he emerged as one of the Yankees' World Series heroes in 1949, Allie lived an insular life. He was, and still is, a difficult man to know, and his family respects his moods.

Never a talkative man, The Chief, as he is known among his teammates, inadvertently discourages bosom friendships. Allie prefers to keep his own counsel. He continues to be something of a loner among the Yankees, although compared to the sulky rookie he was in his Cleveland days, Reynolds has become positively jovial.

In those days, Allie had a violent temper. He's learned to control it, but there was a time he'd sulk for weeks at some misfortune that had happened to him on the field. "I guess my Indian traits kept coming out," Allie says. "To some extent,

I'm still that way, but now I'm inclined to take bad breaks as normal occurrences in the life of a guy who's trying to earn a living in a hazardous business."

Allie doesn't pretend, however, that he wasn't deeply hurt by the "Reynolds-Page" and "The Vanishing American" gags of 1949. Allie could find nothing funny in the monotony of his incomplete games and the way Page mopped up for him. He still looks back on that year as an extended nightmare.

"That season was my most miserable year," he says. "Complete games are as important to me as they are to any other starting pitcher, but people were acting as though I liked what was going on.

"The whispers couldn't help get back to me," Allie recalls bitterly. "I was being accused of being a pitcher who wanted out after I had my lead and my five innings out of the way. That way, I'd get my win, but if the game was lost I couldn't be charged with the defeat. How could I answer a charge like that? Nobody ever said it to me directly, and it seemed as though it was correct.

"Nobody wanted to pitch complete games any more than I did," Allie says. "I tried to figure out why I couldn't. I wasn't losing my stuff. I wasn't tiring. I talked to Jim (Coach Jim Turner) about it and he thought maybe I was relaxing unconsciously when I got ahead. That could have been it because I'd always tried to pace myself while pitching. Jim said maybe I ought to get mad at the fellows I was pitching at. Maybe he was right. Maybe not. When I get knocked out, I'm not mad at the other guys; I'm mad at myself."

Allie has taken on polish off the field as well as on it since coming to New York. He was never clothes-conscious until he noted how well most of the Yankee players dress. Now he keeps apace of his teammates as something of a fashion plate. He favors sport jackets, loud ties, and sports shirts of lemon-yellow.

Around the house, he's a T-shirt Charley. He may read a Western or spend the morning practicing casting in the backyard with Allie Dale. Like his father, the son loves to fish and hunt and has had no trouble wangling parental permission to go out on his own with a rifle.

The day Allie pitches, particularly, is a lounging one for him, although he has no fixed routine. Many pitchers go through a regular routine the day they are to work. Except for eating lightly, Reynolds acts as he does on any other morning.

Ordinarily, Allie is the kind of man who'll eat anything that doesn't bite him first, especially if it's sweet. He has one of the most vigorously exercised sweet-teeth in baseball. He thinks nothing of eating triple helpings of ice cream between games of a double-header. Only the fear that he'll balloon from his best playing weight (190 pounds, which he carries compactly on his six-foot frame) keeps him from having pies and cakes with every meal.

When the season is over, however, Allie indulges himself in all his favorite foods. He gets rid of excess weight easily, for he spends much of the off-season quail hunting. He may have to devote less of his time to hunting in future off-seasons, however, for he has recently become a partner in an import-export firm.

For Mrs. Reynolds, the off-season is the one time she can relax. While Allie conceals his feelings about baseball behind his Indian's mask-like calm, Earlene, who has no Indian blood, is apparently the family's safety-valve. She lives and dies with her husband's every pitch, yet she tries to be at the Stadium each time Allie works when the Yankees are home.

The 1949 season, she says, was her worst. The heat of the pennant race made her a nervous wreck. Before the Yanks finally clinched the flag, she had become afflicted with shingles, a nervous ailment that reflects itself in a skin rash.

Mrs. Reynolds always seems to take her husband's victories and defeats harder than he does, at least on the surface. If he pitches well, she tries to wear the same items of clothing the next time he takes the mound.

"I wish I could take baseball as lightly as Eileen Henrich, Tommy's wife did," Earlene admits. "She never even knew or cared what the score was, or whether Tommy did well. I can't wait until I can talk to Allie about it, but I never do until he brings up the game. I keep a pretty fair box-score and always bring it home after a game. That gives us the chance to go over what has happened.

"Maybe Allie's kidding me, but he tells me it helps him a lot to look at my box-score and replay the game off it."

If Allie and his wife insist that his 1-0 victory over Don Newcombe and the Dodgers in the opening game of the 1949 World Series was the turning point in his pitching career, the evidence backs them up. The Chief had a 16-12 season in 1950, but with 14 complete games, compared to his four full-time jobs in 1949. Obviously, he no longer was the Vanishing American.

Reynolds pitched another classic in the World Series that fall, beating the Phillies in the second game at Shibe Park by 2 to 1 in 10 innings on Joe DiMaggio's home run. Allie would not have been scored upon at all had not a single by Eddie Waitkus in the fifth taken a freak hop past Jerry Coleman at second.

The Chief was the only pitcher of the Yanks to make more than one appearance in the sweep over the Phils. After a muff of a fly ball put Eddie Ford, the rookie southpaw, on a spot in the ninth inning of the final game, Manager Stengel called on Reynolds to face Stan Lopata with two out, two on and the Yanks ahead, 5 to 2. It took Allie exactly four pitches to fan Lopata and wrap up the Series.

Although Reynolds reported to the Phoenix training camp in 1951 with bone chips rattling around in his right elbow, he was destined to have his greatest season from this dismal beginning. He again won 17 games, this time with 16 complete efforts and pitched two no-hit, no-run games, something which no other American Leaguer ever did in one season. Johnny VanderMeer, with his successive no-hitters in 1938 for the Reds against the Braves and the Dodgers, was the only pitcher ever to come up with two no-hitters before in the same year.

There was a story behind each of Reynolds' no-hitters; his first was against Cleveland, the team which had traded him to the Yankees and his second, fashioned against the Red Sox in the opening game of a double header at the Stadium on September 28, assured the Yanks of no worse than a tie for the 1951 pennant. The latter was the game in which Yogi Berra, with two out in the ninth, dropped a foul pop hit by the dangerous Ted Williams.

Berra's error put Reynolds distinctly on the spot, for he had to get past Williams to protect his no-hitter. Again Ted raised a foul fly near the Yankee dugout. This time Yogi

88

caught the ball and the Chief caught Yogi to make sure he held on to it.

Reynolds was beaten by the Giants in the opening game of the World Series but came back to win the fourth game and even the Series at two-all. And the Yanks never lost another game.

Reynolds had the best season of his career in 1952, even though it wasn't marked by any no-hitters. He won 20 games for the first time in his life and led the American league pitchers in strikeouts and had the best earned run average in the league.

Beaten in the opening game of the World Series when the Dodgers fielded sensationally behind Joe Black, Chief Wahoo came back in the fourth game to win, shutting out Black and the Brooks with four hits. He struck out 10 in this game, three times slipping a third strike past Jackie Robinson and twice getting the dangerous Campanella on strikes.

Allie also was credited with the winning of the seventh and deciding game at Ebbets Field when he went to the rescue of Lopat with the bases filled in the fourth. He allowed one run until Major Ralph Houk batted for him in the seventh, but Bob Kuzava's later relief hurling and Billy Martin's sensational catch of Robinson's wind-blown pop fly were important factors in the fourth straight World Series victory of the Yankees.

CHAPTER VI

THE JUNK MAN
(Eddie Lopat)

BY TOM MEANY

Eddie Lopat is probably the only ball player George Weiss ever apologized for buying. And, irrelevantly, it should be noted that George never apologized for any ball players he sold, although there were many who felt that he should have. Lopat came to the Yankees just before the spring training season opened in 1948, via a trade which sent Bill Wight, a left handed pitcher with a deadly motion to first base, and Aaron Robinson, a long-ball hitting catcher, to the White Sox.

Lopat had labored four years for the White Sox with a so-so record. He won 50 and lost 49, not bad for a pitcher working with a chronic second division club, but not exactly stimulating, either.

Weiss was having lunch in the clubhouse at Sunshine Park, the homey little race track at Oldsmar, Florida, in 1948, when he felt impelled to explain to a writer his reasons for picking up Lopat.

"We won the pennant and the World Series last fall," said George, "and I think maybe we could repeat this year without help but it is good for a ball club to make changes. Yogi Berra is coming along now and we can afford to give up Robinson. It peps up the whole ball club to know that we have another starting pitcher and haven't hurt ourselves any in making the trade."

Did George think Lopat could be a starter with the Yankees?

"Sure," he replied cheerfully. "Did you notice his record with the White Sox for the last four years? He averaged about one walk every four innings. Any pitcher who can get the ball over the plate can win for us."

Lopat made Weiss look good with 17 wins that season, even though it was Cleveland who won the pennant. Eddie didn't start too well but he was pitching good ball at the end of the year and he has come on to be one of the club's aces, as well as the outstanding pitcher of the 1951 World Series with two victories over the Giants.

It was characteristic of Lopat's career that Weiss should have felt it necessary to explain that he was a better pitcher than met the eye. When Billy Evans, the former American League owner, was president of the Southern League, he had the very dickens of a time trying to convince major league owners that the stocky southpaw could win in the big apple.

"Lopat was pitching for Little Rock," explained Evans, "and I saw a lot of his work. After being a big league umpire for over 20 years, I felt I was a good judge of a pitcher but nobody wanted to take my word for Lopat.

"I finally got the White Sox to take him but I had to do quite a selling job. And the price was hardly flattering to Eddie.

The Sox bought him for $12,500, but only paid $2500 down, the other $10,000 to be paid when, and if, Lopat made good."

The tendency to underrate Lopat is a common one and nowhere is it more prevalent than among American League batters, who contemptuously refer to him as "The Junk Man." The popular belief is that Eddie has no fast ball. The dumpy left hander insists that he has a fast ball but somehow he manages to keep it a secret.

Lopat uses his fast ball as window dressing. He lets the batters look at it, but he never intentionally puts it close enough to the plate for them to hit. The balls that Eddie pitches within range of hitters are a wide variety of stuff— slow balls, sinkers, curves, change-of-pace. The batter, having looked at the fast ball pitched tantalizingly out of his reach, finds that the slow stuff appears much slower.

The secret of Lopat's success is, of course, his control. Not only does Eddie walk far fewer hitters than the average pitcher but he rarely gets "behind" on them, permitting the count to go in their favor. He can pitch to spots—and nearly every hitter has a weakness. Eddie doesn't strike out many—he is content to let his fielders work for him.

It was a long, rough road for Lopat before the glib tongue of Evans convinced the White Sox that the southpaw would be worth a gamble—and $2500 was the limit the Sox gambled on him. Eddie started out as a left-handed hitting first baseman with Greensburg in the Pennsylvania State League in 1937. Seven years, five leagues and eight clubs later he arrived in Chicago.

Lopat played 34 games at first base for Greensburg before the management became convinced that a first sacker hitting

.229 would be better off some place else. "Some place else" turned out to be Jeanerette, Louisiana, in the Evangeline League. The .229 batting average convinced Eddie he would be better off some place else, too, and in his case, some place else turned out to be the pitcher's box.

Eddie didn't win a game as he finished up the 1937 season for Jeanerette but he won a dozen the next season and then his travels and his travails commenced. Kilgore, Texas; Salina, Kansas; Shreveport, Louisiana; and Oklahoma City were some of the stops Lopat made before settling down at Little Rock.

And Lopat really settled down at Little Rock, too. He made his winter home there and went into business. He also won 19 games there in 1943 for Willis Hudlin, himself once a pitcher of parts with Cleveland, and then was sold to the White Sox.

Among the many bum raps hung on Lopat was that he took things too easily, was too nonchalant on the mound. This simply isn't so. Eddie is a good competitor but he makes pitching look easy. He explains this by saying that he spent hours practicing his control and found it easier to throw slow stuff to a target than fast stuff.

Lopat had only three good seasons among his years in the minors—his 12-7 mark with Jeanerette in 1938, a 16-9 season with Longview in the East Texas League the following year and his 19-10 record with Little Rock in 1943. And in the American League, he has had only one losing season, a 10-13 mark with the White Sox in 1945. Eddie apparently gets better as he goes along, as witness his high-water mark of 1951, 21-9.

When Lopat learned he had been traded to the Yankees, he privately thought that the champs were getting the short end of the deal. When his first few outings were unimpressive, a scribe traveling with the club wrote a treatise that Eddie was a "hot weather" pitcher and predicted when the sun shone, Lopat, too, would shine.

This was erroneous but it sounded good and Lopat used it as an alibi to explain any off-games in the spring of the year. He pitched a two-hitter against the Red Sox in the second game of the 1951 season in chilly April and held the Giants to one earned run in 18 innings in the World Series in murky October. That was hardly the type of pitching expected from a fellow who was supposed to need warm weather.

The truth of the matter is that a guy born on New York's East Side, on Avenue A, and raised around 90th Street and Lexington Avenue, is immune to low temperatures. Eddie can recall playing "stick-ball" in the snow. The old time neighbors still remember Lopat as a kid who could hit the ball a mile in stick-ball.

Lopat has developed as a pitcher since joining the Yankees. He isn't winning more games simply because the club he is now pitching for is stronger than the White Sox of Jimmy Dykes' era but because he has improved his talents.

When Lopat came to the Yanks he had a two-way curve, a change of pace and what is laughingly known as his fast one. In his second season with the Yankees, 1949, under Casey Stengel, Eddie began experimenting with a screw-ball and a knuckler.

The chunky Pole is constantly working on his equipment. He frequently warms up on days when he isn't pitching, always working on new and old deliveries, even while pitching batting practice. Eddie believes that the winter baseball school

94

he has been running in Florida is also of great assistance to him in his experiments with new pitches and his improving of the old ones.

Lopat calls pitching a guessing game. "If I can get the batters to guess with me, I figure I've got an edge," he explains. "I've got five or six different deliveries I can throw, so the odds on their guessing the right pitch are against them."

Although Lopat has an easy motion, it is an unusual one and many a batter has thrown his bat away after popping up or dribbling a soft one to the infield, muttering that he has been hitting at Eddie's delivery, instead of at the ball.

Like most of the other Yankees, Lopat has been in four straight World Series and he has yet to lose a game in the battles for the pot o'gold. He scored one rather sloppy victory over the Dodgers in 1949. Eddie was 6-0 going into the sixth when the Dodgers piled into him for four runs after two were out. Allie Reynolds came in and protected the lead.

It was in '51 that Lopat really starred in the Series. The surprising Giants, in the greatest stretch run in baseball history, won 38 of 47 games to take the National League pennant. Manager Leo Durocher pulled a surprise starter, Dave Koslo, in the opener at Yankee Stadium and the left hander beat the Yanks 5 to 1.

The red-hot Giants were in a fair way to take it all then, precisely as the miracle Braves of 1914 had. The Braves staged a great rally to come from last place to first in two and a half months and then beat Connie Mack's mighty Athletics four straight in the Series. Hot as the Giants were, Lopat cooled them off by beating Larry Jansen by 3 to 1 in the second game to even the Series at one-all.

Lopat also won the sixth game, this by a score of 13 to 1.

This game was played at the Polo Grounds and some of the experts thought Stengel was taking a chance to pitch Eddie with his slow stuff in a park where the walls are invitingly close.

"The fences are short only at the foul lines," explained Casey afterward, "and I knew the Giants couldn't pull Eddie. Lopat knows how to pitch. He lets the hitters supply all the power. There wasn't a fly hit to right field all day and Gene Woodling in left and Joe DiMaggio in center had eight chances between them."

Lopat had arm trouble in 1952 and won only ten games but he was a great help to Stengel in the stretch drive. Half of his victories were against first-division clubs. In the four pennant-winning seasons of the Yankees, 1948-'50-'51-'52, Steady Eddie built up a 38-19 collective record against the three foes who shared the first division with the Yankees. That's a two-to-one ratio against the contenders.

This ability to knock off the strong teams was never more in evidence than in 1950 when Lopat won six decisions without a defeat against the Indians. When Eddie continued in '51 where he had left off, it assumed the proportions of a civic scandal in Cleveland.

An enterprising Ohio statistician, whose tastes were somewhat morbid, discovered that Lopat's first two victories over the Indians gave him a string of 10 straight over the Tribe. They hadn't beaten the junk man since June 17, 1949. The Cleveland *Press* jokingly suggested that there was something of black magic in Eddie's charmed life against the Indians.

It is always a mistake to joke about baseball in Cleveland, where the fans are at least as fanatical as those of **Flat-bush**. There was hysteria in the air when Lopat came to town with the Yankees to face the Tribe in a night game at the vast Municipal Stadium on the shores of Lake Erie on June 4.

The Cleveland fans were ready for Eddie. After the Yanks had been retired in the top half of the first inning, Lopat went to the mound, threw his warm-up pitches to Yogi Berra, and signalled that he was ready to face the first Indian batter. Before a ball could be thrown, however, a customer vaulted the railing, ran to the mound and hit Eddie with a live, snarling, clawing black cat!

In addition to being scratched, Lopat was beaten, for the Tribe broke the jinx by knocking him out in two innings. The most remarkable thing about this outburst was the calm with which Lopat took it. Several of the players, Indians as well as Yankees, were indignant. "If a fan ever did that to me, I'd punch him right in the nose," declared Al Rosen, Cleveland third baseman.

Lopat didn't punch anybody in the nose but he cooled Cleveland's pennant hopes exactly three months later to the day at Yankee Stadium. The pennant race was as close as the next second and the popular assumption was that this game, in which Lopat faced Bob Lemon before a crowd of better than 40,000 on a Monday afternoon, would have a vital bearing on the race.

"We could lose today and still have a chance to win the pennant," said one of the Cleveland players before the game, "but the Yankees can't win the pennant unless they win this game."

An error by Phil Rizzuto on a difficult chance hit by Jim

Hegan led to a Cleveland run in the sixth, tying the score. The Yanks had tallied in the previous inning on a ground rule double by Bobby Brown and Rizzuto's single.

With one out in the ninth, DiMaggio scratched a questionable hit off Rosen's glove. Gene Woodling sent Joe to third with a single to right and Bobby Brown was intentionally passed to fill the bases. This strategy by Cleveland manager Al Lopez later was hotly debated by the second guessers who argued that it put a strain on Lemon, since a base on balls meant the ball game.

"What a spot this would be for Bill Veeck's midget," quipped a press box tenant.

"Well," retorted his companion, pointing to the five-foot, six-inch Rizzuto, smallest player in the majors, "the Yanks have the next best thing."

Tiny Phil laid down a perfect squeeze bunt, so well placed that no play was possible, and DiMaggio came home with the winning run.

The victory gave Lopat a lifetime record of 33 victories in 41 decisions with Cleveland, a real Indian sign if you'll pardon the pun. When asked for the secret of his success against the Tribe, Lopat cheerfully admitted that there wasn't any.

"As I say," he explained, "this is a guessing game and they've been guessing wrong against me most of the time. When they guess wrong, I'm still working; if they guess right, I'm taking a bath."

It must be admitted that Eddie guesses right more often than not and does most of his bathing after the game, when it is most enjoyable.

CHAPTER VII

THE MUSCLE MAN
(Yogi Berra)

BY BEN EPSTEIN

There was an informal party in a private dining room on the third floor of Toots Shor's restaurant on West 51st Street the night of January 21, 1952. The members of the New York chapter of baseball writers had gathered to honor Charley Segar, one of their former members who had been named by Commissioner Ford C. Frick to the post of secretary-treasurer of baseball.

Among those called to the microphone to say a few words was Yogi Berra, the doughty Yankee catcher, who was wearing a necktie for the occasion. Berra had joined the Yanks at the end of the 1946 season, the year in which Segar had resigned from the staff of the *Daily Mirror* to head the National League Service Bureau. Their paths therefore had never crossed back in the days when Segar covered the Yanks for the *Mirror*.

"Well, Charley, I don't know what to say," began Yogi. "I never met you, I guess."

There were roars of laughter and another Berraism was born. It didn't bother Yogi any more than the American League pitchers bother him.

"All I know about Berra," remarked one of the writers present, "is that people laugh at him all year 'round and he winds up in a World Series every fall. He must have something."

There was a lot of truth in that remark. In his first six full seasons with the Yankees, Yogi was in five World Series. It is fairly patent that the young man has something and that that something is valuable to the Yankees. That this fact is recognized elsewhere than in New York was indicated when the Baseball Writers Association of America voted Yogi the most valuable player in the American League in 1951.

Casey Stengel's voice rasped through the lobby of the Hotel Del Prado on Chicago's South Side one night in 1950 during the final Western swing of the Yankees. His cement mixer tones growled through the entire structure and probably had a change of pace effect upon the Lake Michigan waters two blocks away.

A mixed audience of players, baseball writers and guests listened with the amused attention which only a commentary from Casey can command. Stengel produces the world's most irregular double talk, a combination of wit, facial gestures and pantomime.

Nearly always there is a method to Stengel's conversational madness. Almost invariably the Yankee manager aims his talk, purposefully, at one individual. This time the target, Lawrence Peter (Yogi) Berra, squatted in a cushioned chair and needed no lawyer to enable him to get the drift. Berra heard the mention of money and his passionate attachment for the beloved buck brought forth immediate attention.

"If you listen to what I got to say," blared Casey, fisting his hands for emphasis, "I'll make you a $500,000-a-year catcher." Stengel's face contorted into a wrinkled web. "That's what I said—a half-million bucks. You want to know how? Well,—"

But Yogi interrupted in his Berra basso profoundo. "Sure, I know. Invent (*sic*) in oil like you do and get good tips on the market. I hear you got more money than Del Webb and Dan Topping put together."

Stengel brushed off Yogi's remarks and continued with his lecture. "Just do what you can do a little more often and I'll personally see to it that you get every penny you ask for next spring."

It was an unusual pep-talk but then Stengel is an unusual manager. He was needling Berra into going all out in the ensuing pennant drive.

Berra, of course, delivered and he also remembered. Came the winter of 1950-51 and Yogi chopped a cipher off Stengel's extravagant guarantee and asked for $50,000 for 1951. He settled for $30,000 but the thought of the 50 G's continues to buzz in the head of the man who possesses what the National Association of Women Artists voted "the most down-to-earth face in America."

Berra's worth drew a wistful remark from Mel Ott when the Yankees faced his Oakland Acorns on the Coast in March, 1951. "Yogi is still as pretty as ever," grinned Ottie, "and his ball playing is prettier than ever. Remember, I'm the guy who saw him first. When I was managing the Giants in 1945, I offered $50,000 for him and I figured he someday would develop into a $500,000 catcher. That's what he'd bring on the market today."

Ott's evaluation of Berra's worth at a half-million dollars may have been mere coincidence, but maybe Stengel wasn't kidding that night in the lobby of the Del Prado after all.

"When I first saw Yogi the Giants were playing an exhibition game at the New London, Connecticut, Naval Base," recalled Ott. "All I could see was that little squat catcher who seemed so right because he was doing everything all wrong. I know it doesn't make sense but he stopped everything behind the bat and swung at everything in front of it. He made two hits on two wild pitches."

Ott decided to talk things over with Larry MacPhail, who, along with Webb and Topping, had purchased the Yankees that spring. He visited Larry the next day and offered $50,000 for Berra. There was a moment of blankness on MacPhail's face until Mel explained that Berra was the little catcher who was up in New London awaiting his discharge from the Navy. That was all the hint MacPhail needed.

"Oh, yes," nodded Larry, sparring for time. "That little catcher. You like him, eh? Well, I don't know. I'll have to check with my farm officials but I think we may be able to swing a deal."

Ott never heard from MacPhail again because Larry started an investigation of his own. When he found that Berra's experience in the Yankee chain had been one year at their Norfolk, Virginia, farm club, he immediately ordered Berra to proceed to New York.

"I wanted to get a look at this kid who sold Ott a bill of goods on the strength of one ball game—and a $50,000 bill of goods at that," explained MacPhail.

A few days later, Berra, in his Navy blues, waddled into MacPhail's Fifth Avenue offices, and succeeded in frightening his first baseball executive. "He reminded me of the bottom man of a bankrupt acrobatic team," recalled MacPhail.

When Yogi barked, "You wanna see me, mister?" MacPhail would have sold him for fifty cents. MacPhail, however, was a good businessman as well as a sound baseball man. He talked matters over with his scouts and decided that Berra, who had been acquired for practically nothing, was deserving of further inspection.

Berra became Yankee property on payment of a $500 bonus on the advice of Johnny Schulte, then Yankee coach and bullpen catcher. Johnny had seen Berra in his native St. Louis and he knew the Cardinals were interested in the boy.

That $500 bonus may well be one of the shrewdest investments the Yankees ever made. In his seventh full year as a Bomber, Berra in 1953 is one of the game's best catchers. At 28 his skill and power is slowly but surely moving him into the same class with the Dickeys, the Cochranes, the Hartnetts, the Schalks and the Lopezes. In a word, Yogi has class.

Berra has shown power against lefthanded pitchers as well as righthanders, his throwing accuracy has steadily improved and he has confidence in his own catching know-how. And Yogi has something which only a very few of the catching greats, past or present, boasted. He can run, instantly losing his outward appearance of lumbering when the need for speed arises.

"I didn't play all those years of soccer for nuthin'," explains Berra. "I can get there, if I gotta."

The improvement of Berra, although constant, was no

overnight job. It required the formula so often stressed by New York's late Mayor LaGuardia—patience and fortitude. In the 1947 World Series against the Dodgers, Yogi had to be benched after the Dodgers drew abreast and a steadier catcher utilized to save the day. First Sherman Lollar and then Aaron Robinson replaced Berra in the Series, ironically enough, in which Yogi became the first player in World Series history to deliver a home run as a pinch-hitter.

Berra was understandably jittery in this Series and the speed of the Dodgers did nothing to ameliorate it. It was said before the Series that Brooklyn would steal Yogi's glove, mask and protector. They didn't quite do that although, in the fourth game, a good throw by Berra in the ninth inning would have nailed pinch-runner Al Gionfriddo trying to steal second, ended the game and given Floyd (Bill) Bevens the first no-hitter in Series history.

Berra's knees actually shook during the Series, a knocking which Joe DiMaggio swore he not only saw but heard from away out yonder in center field. Yogi's comment on his anatomical shivers merely multiplied his mates' admiration for him.

"Your knees would shake, too," he confessed, "if you had to catch in a World Series. I was too scared to do any good. I was scared when I pinch-hit a homer and the papers said I was the first player to ever do anything like that. Is that on the level?"

It was equally on the level that Berra, instead of cracking under the ridicule, had the Heaven-given gift of immunity to all barbs. He came back to become the first-string catcher of the Yankees in 1948. "I ain't nervous no more," Yogi insisted fervently, if ungrammatically. "I made an unassisted double play last year, something not many other catchers could do. I'm learning how to catch. And don't worry about my throwing. I was throwing rocks all winter in my back yard."

Berra improved in 1948 but it was in 1949 that he took his biggest stride forward. When the Yankees cleaned out the clubhouse brass, firing Bucky Harris and his coaches, Charley Dressen and Red Corriden, Berra felt as if he had lost three close friends. Yet the new deal in the Bronx was to sweep in the man who did the most for Berra—Bill Dickey.

Although Dickey also coaches at first base for Manager Casey Stengel, it was taken for granted that his main job would be to tutor Berra. And, as Casey said to Bill, "If you quit, no hard feelings."

Dickey got his first look at Berra at Miller Huggins Field in St. Petersburg in spring training of 1949. It was about the third day of training and Yogi worked behind the plate in batting practice for about 15 minutes. Dickey parked his car, tied his dog to a fire hydrant and settled into some sort of trance as he watched Berra. A dozen writers, knowing the reason for the intense examination, watched Bill watch Yogi. One of the bravest inquired, "See anything?"

There was a moment of concentrated silence by Dickey and then a smile. "That Berra has the makings of a good catcher," he said. "I can't say a great one but I wouldn't be surprised if he is even that some day. Right now, he does just about everything wrong but I was warned about that. But nobody told me that he could move—really hurry—and that's the main idea. I believe I can get him to throw all right once he learns where to throw the ball from. I know he can hit, for I've seen him pull an outside ball a mile."

Instructing Berra became almost an obsession with Dickey,

who worked with him hour after hour as though it were a daily challenge. Bill started from scratch. Yogi was taught to take a position, the receiving of the ball, shifting his feet, throwing to all bases, chasing pop flies against the dugouts and the screen, fielding bunts, backing up plays at first and third, tagging the runner, hiding the signs, etc. And the most important of all, to keep everlastingly hustling. Berra had a habit of day-dreaming occasionally, of falling asleep between pitches.

Berra's stubby fingers created unexpected trouble. The pitchers couldn't see his abbreviated digits. "Why don't you grow yourself a pair of hands?" one of them unfeelingly asked. To ease the problem Yogi painted his fingers with iodine. "No help," said one of his battery-mates. "It looks like your wrists are bleeding." The word is now that Berra uses his mitts sparingly in giving signs and concentrates on other movements to transmit the signals.

Such a finished product was Berra when the 1951 season rolled around that Bucky Harris, who had Yogi first, declared, "Berra has achieved the impossible. I always knew that Yogi would develop into a great hitter but nobody ever figured he'd be able to run the whole show from behind the bat. Have you noticed that such pitchers as Vic Raschi, Ed Lopat and Allie Reynolds seldom shake him off? He must know the score. It's a miracle."

Harris' opinion received strong support from Raschi. "Yogi called every pitch in my 1-0 shutout against the Phillies in the opening game of the 1950 World Series," said the big righthander. "Don't sell Berra short in judging the strength and weakness of a batter. He not only remembers the club-house briefings but he is pretty cute in rattling a guy at the plate. I don't know what he tells him, or what he is saying when he is barbering with the umpires but I'm sure it has nothing to do with the next pitch."

Berra will not elaborate on what he chats about when he seeks to engage rival batters in conversation.

"I say a few things, but nothing mean, y'understand," said Yogi. "Just how they're doin' and that I hope they have a good year—but not against us. I might tell 'em that a certain pitcher is a little wild today and not to forget to be a little careful. That keeps 'em from diggin' in too much and makes 'em press."

Here Yogi made a gesture of shushing his lips as though such standard operating procedure were highly unethical. "Sometimes it works, too," he added.

The fine catching of Berra is a tribute to Dickey, who was an outstanding catcher himself. Yogi sums up his own tribute to Bill in what is perhaps the most often quoted of all the Berraisms. "He is learning me all his experience," he declared.

Berra came from a section of St. Louis predominantly Italian in its population and known locally as "The Hill." It also produced Joe Garagiola, the catcher who played so well for the Cardinals in the 1946 World Series and who in 1951 was traded to Pittsburgh. They were playmates on the various kid teams around the Hill and Joe swears that, in an informal football game, Yogi scored a touchdown with such violence that he bent an iron post.

Both Garagiola and Berra received tryouts from the Cardinals. This was in the summer of 1942 and while Branch Rickey, then the resident genius of the Red Bird organization, approved a bonus of three or four hundred dollars for Joe, Yogi was told that he wouldn't be paid for his autograph. Some months later, after Rickey had shifted his brains to Brooklyn, he got in touch with Berra but by then Schulte had grabbed him for the Yankees.

It was Jack McGuire, a son of a major league scout and an outfielder who was with the Giants and Pirates in 1951, who gave Berra his nickname of Yogi. Asked why he bestowed such a handle on the stumpy Berra, McGuire replied that it was because he walked like a Yogi, an answer fully as baffling as any Berra ever has given.

After being sent to Norfolk in the Piedmont League, where he distinguished himself by batting in a total of 23 runs in two successive days, Berra went into the Navy and spent D-Day fishing bodies out of the surf off the coast of Normandy. He was back in New London in 1945 when he caught Mel Ott's eye, as related.

The big moment in Berra's life came when he met Miss Carmen Short and shyly had his friend, Garagiola, arrange for a date to go to the movies. The movie date blossomed into a marriage on January 26, 1949, with Garagiola as the best man. The couple were blessed with Lawrence, Junior, who has Carmen's charming beauty and Yogi's muscles, which seems to be an unbeatable combination.

In 1948, the Yankees noticed that Berra went around with a sort of moonstruck expression. His catching was improving, his batting was powerful but when the club was Pullman-ing from town to town, Yogi was gazing into space. Even his favorite comic books no longer held his interest.

The secret came out one night on a train when a photo

of Carmen fell out of Yogi's pocket. He confessed that it was his sweetheart.

"As soon as we get to Washington and Phil Rizzuto introduces me to that jewelry salesman there, we're gonna get engaged," he admitted, and then added cautiously, "if the prices of rings is right."

It is characteristic of Berra that the printing of this story in the papers at the time was the first inkling Miss Short, or Yogi's parents, had of his matrimonial intentions.

When Berra finally came out of the Navy, he was assigned to finish out the 1946 season with the Yankee farm at Newark. He joined the club in Rochester and the clubhouse boy tried to issue a raggedy uniform to Berra, believing him some youngster who was reporting for a try out. "Gimme a decent uniform," said Yogi, "I'm a regular."

Never were truer words spoken, for Berra was a regular from then on, batting .314 for the Bears and hitting 15 home runs as he finished out the year with them, and was called into Yankee Stadium for a tryout.

With the Bears, Berra roomed with Bobby Brown, who had the nickname of Golden Boy because of the bonus the Yankees had paid for his services. The infielder, who was studying for the medical degree he received in the winter of 1950-51, lugged a forbidding looking medical tome to bed with him each night, a book which was as bulky as the phone directory of a fair-sized metropolis. Each bed-time Yogi curled up with such current comic books as he could lay his hands on.

One night Berra observed that Brown no longer had the medical book. He asked Bobby what had happened.

"I finished it," explained Brown.

"Yeah?" queried the interested Yogi. "How did it come out?"

Brown explained the book, as best he could to Berra. Like all the players, Bobby is genuinely fond of the stocky catcher. "I'll try to make it plain and simple, Yogi," said Bobby. "It was a book which embraced both therapeutics and pharmacology."

"I get it," snappily retorted Berra. "Something like Buck Rogers uses when he gets in a jam."

Berra's quotations are highly prized but there is a suspicion that Yogi makes many of them up just for the laughs, for he is by no means the clown he pretends to be. Some, of course, are honest slips, such as the remark he made when admirers from the Hill presented him with a "night" at Sportsman's Park in his native St. Louis and showered him with gifts.

"I want to thank everybody who made this night necessary," he boomed into the public address system.

One of Berra's least known but highly valued remarks was about the water cooler in the dugout of the St. Louis Browns, which, when Yogi took a drink from it, was in a somewhat dilapidated condition.

"Why don't you guys tell the owners to break down and buy some new water?" he angrily asked.

Frank Scott, who was traveling secretary for the Yankees until 1951 and now acts as a business representative for several of the players, including Berra, swears that Yogi demanded to have his room changed in a certain hotel because he didn't like the Murphy bed.

"I ain't gonna sleep standing up," he insisted.

Yankees play in Puerto Rico, Venezuela and Cuba before settling down at St. Pete.

"If I was writing, I'd take notes on everything Yogi says," declared Bobby. "Believe me, he's going to be a star some day and these remarks of his will be treasured. He has amazing power at the plate, more than you yet realize. In batting practice with the Bears, we used to hit balls for distance, the fellow who hit the longest ball getting free cokes. Yogi won every time."

During that same trip, Berra got in some good licks against the Dodgers, then managed by the shortly to be suspended Leo Durocher. The Lip pitched lefthanders in an effort to stop Berra but Yogi hit them as hard as he hit the righthanders.

"The only way to stop that barrel," declared the Lip, "is to frisk him for extra muscles." It was an appropriate crack, too, since, because of unsettled political conditions in Venezuela, nobody was allowed in the ball park in Caracas without being searched by the police.

Among Berra's friends from the Hill in St. Louis is a young man who has a position of some responsibility with the office of the Collector of Internal Revenue. Yogi sought his help in preparing his income tax in 1949, at a time when he was holding out and exchanging heated communiqués with General Manager Weiss.

Berra, after receiving assistance in preparing the return for the year of 1948, was then given the form for preparing his estimated income return for 1949.

"How much are you going to make this year?" asked the friend.

"That's none of your business—yet," Yogi told the man from the tax office.

Despite Scott's protestations of authenticity, this remark has yet to be accepted by the A.A.U.

Berra reported to the Yankees in the last week of the 1946 season, fresh from Newark where he had served as catcher and part-time outfielder. He was still in blue—serge, instead of Navy—and was sporting a bandaged wrist. It was the result of crashing into a fence in pursuit of a fly ball "because the lights didn't burn good enough."

The Yanks were managed by Johnny Neun, who that month had succeeded Dickey who had succeeded Joe McCarthy in May. Thus the man who is now the chief trouble-shooter for General Manager George Weiss was the first of three managers to realize that Berra was the beginning of something he couldn't explain. For that matter, neither could Neun's successors, Harris or Stengel. Berra looks awkward but he delivers.

In two days with the Yanks, Berra smashed home runs into the right-field stands at the Stadium, one on a high-outside pitch, the other on a high-inside pitch by way of demonstrating his complete separation from the orthodox.

Yogi's second homer cracked the mask of DiMaggio. The Yankee Clipper decided to take a "complete" look at Berra when the team assembled at the 125th Street station to take a train for Boston. DiMag studied Yogi and Berra, puffing away on a mooched cigarette, returned the compliment.

Finally Joe shook his head and laughed good naturedly. Yogi laughed right back and muttered, "I can hit homers, too."

Brown, Berra's Newark roommate, never ceased trying to sell the writers traveling with the Yankees a bill of goods on the catcher in the spring of 1947, a spring which saw the

"I finished it," explained Brown.

"Yeah?" queried the interested Yogi. "How did it come out?"

Brown explained the book, as best he could to Berra. Like all the players, Bobby is genuinely fond of the stocky catcher. "I'll try to make it plain and simple, Yogi," said Bobby. "It was a book which embraced both therapeutics and pharmacology."

"I get it," snappily retorted Berra. "Something like Buck Rogers uses when he gets in a jam."

Berra's quotations are highly prized but there is a suspicion that Yogi makes many of them up just for the laughs, for he is by no means the clown he pretends to be. Some, of course, are honest slips, such as the remark he made when admirers from the Hill presented him with a "night" at Sportsman's Park in his native St. Louis and showered him with gifts.

"I want to thank everybody who made this night necessary," he boomed into the public address system.

One of Berra's least known but highly valued remarks was about the water cooler in the dugout of the St. Louis Browns, which, when Yogi took a drink from it, was in a somewhat dilapidated condition.

"Why don't you guys tell the owners to break down and buy some new water?" he angrily asked.

Frank Scott, who was traveling secretary for the Yankees until 1951 and now acts as a business representative for several of the players, including Berra, swears that Yogi demanded to have his room changed in a certain hotel because he didn't like the Murphy bed.

"I ain't gonna sleep standing up," he insisted.

of Carmen fell out of Yogi's pocket. He confessed that it was his sweetheart.

"As soon as we get to Washington and Phil Rizzuto introduces me to that jewelry salesman there, we're gonna get engaged," he admitted, and then added cautiously, "if the prices of rings is right."

It is characteristic of Berra that the printing of this story in the papers at the time was the first inkling Miss Short, or Yogi's parents, had of his matrimonial intentions.

When Berra finally came out of the Navy, he was assigned to finish out the 1946 season with the Yankee farm at Newark. He joined the club in Rochester and the clubhouse boy tried to issue a raggedy uniform to Berra, believing him some youngster who was reporting for a try out. "Gimme a decent uniform," said Yogi, "I'm a regular."

Never were truer words spoken, for Berra was a regular from then on, batting .314 for the Bears and hitting 15 home runs as he finished out the year with them, and was called into Yankee Stadium for a tryout.

With the Bears, Berra roomed with Bobby Brown, who had the nickname of Golden Boy because of the bonus the Yankees had paid for his services. The infielder, who was studying for the medical degree he received in the winter of 1950-51, lugged a forbidding looking medical tome to bed with him each night, a book which was as bulky as the phone directory of a fair-sized metropolis. Each bed-time Yogi curled up with such current comic books as he could lay his hands on.

One night Berra observed that Brown no longer had the medical book. He asked Bobby what had happened.

"Well, let's put it this way," asked the examiner. "How much do you expect to be paid in 1949?"

"More than the Yankees expect to pay me," promptly replied the holdout catcher.

Crazy, eh?

If Yogi was a little crazy at the start of the 1952 season, he couldn't have been blamed. An injury in a spring exhibition game ruined his timing and it took him a long time to get going. He finished strong, however, hitting 30 homers, an all-time high for him and belting two more in the World Series against the Dodgers. The second of these was hit in the sixth game at Ebbets Field and tied up the game, which the Yanks eventually won.

CHAPTER VIII

THE SCOOTER
(Phil Rizzuto)

BY JOE TRIMBLE

Casey Stengel is a lucky man, but not because his petroleum leases and real-estate investments have made him a millionaire. Those windfalls could be due to sound judgment. He is lucky because he blew a chance to avail himself of the talent of Phil Rizzuto back in 1936, and then got another opportunity to ride to glory with the greatest "little" baseball player in history—after a lapse of thirteen years. Few big league managers, after muffing the opportunity to sign an outstanding prospect, get a second chance. Stengel was manager of the Dodgers in 1936 when Rizzuto was booted out of a tryout session and manager of the Yankees in 1949, 1950 1951 and 1952 when the mighty mite carried the New York club to successive world championships. He's like the guy who does a bad job of drilling for water and strikes oil.

Actually, Stengel didn't reject, personally, the seventeen-year-old Rizzuto that summer afternoon many years ago. But the manager was guilty of losing the youngster by reason of his absence. Casey was involved in a feud with the owners of the Brooklyn club and knew that he was going to be fired at the end of the season. He just didn't bother to go to the morning tryout of sandlotters, preferring to leave the appraisals in the hands of others.

A couple of coaches supervised the Ebbets Field session, trying to look over 150 kids in a couple of hours. They, naturally, were taken with the bigger boys and almost completely overlooked such runts as Phil.

"They did give me a lick at bat," the great Yankee shortstop recalls. "But it wasn't much. A big righthanded kid was pitching and his first pitch hit me squarely in the back. It hurt like the devil and the wind was knocked out of me.

"I probably should have gotten out of the batter's box and rested up until the pain left. But I didn't want them to think I was afraid. So I stepped right in again. Then I could hardly swing and, after missing a couple of pitches, I heard one of the coaches say, 'Okay, sonny. That's all. I don't think you'll do, little fellow. Good thing you didn't get hurt bad by that big guy.'"

Perhaps things would have gone differently if Stengel had been present, perhaps not. Casey, a sound judge of talent, doubtless would have taken a look at the kid's fielding, anyway. In later years, it was said that Rizzuto was born to be a star. That may be, but even the brightest star needs a heaven in which to twinkle. Rizzuto also was passed over by scouts from the Boston Red Sox and St. Louis Cardinals that summer because of his size and finally tossed out of the Polo Grounds when he attended a Giant tryout session.

Bill Terry was managing the Giants in those days and, like Stengel, he has been branded in legend. Those who disliked the frosty-dispositioned manager passed along the story, in later years, that Terry had given Phil the heave-ho. But Bill was only as guilty as Stengel—he also was busy elsewhere.

It was Frank (Pancho) Snyder, one of Terry's coaches, who gave Phil the gate without a second look. Pancho, a huge man with the build of a wrestler, had been a catcher in the National League for years—a hard-boiled character who measured ability in ratio to physical proportion.

Snyder, shooing the boy away without even letting him throw or catch a ball, said gruffly, "You're too small, kid. You'll never do. Go home and get yourself a shoeshine box!"

His size was always a source of embarrassment to Rizzuto, from the earliest days he can remember. He was always the littlest kid on the block, the one who was chosen last when the gang picked sides for a ball game or a fight.

Phil, third of four children, was born in Ridgewood, a section of the borough of Brooklyn which is very close to Queens; the adjoining borough as you travel east toward Long Island. His parents, Rose Angotti and Philip Rizzuto, had both been born and reared in the downtown section of the borough, not far from the Brooklyn Bridge. They grew up in the same neighborhood and were married there in 1913.

Mary, the first child, was born a year later and Rose, named after her mother, came along in 1916. She was a twin but the other baby, also a girl, did not survive birth. Papa Rizzuto, then a day-laborer, was not making much money and, in 1917, he tried to improve the living standards of his growing family by taking a steady job. He was hired by the Brooklyn Rapid Transit Company as a trolley-car conductor. His route was from Brooklyn to Queens, from Ridgewood to Richmond Hill, so he moved Mrs. Rizzuto and the girls to Ridge-wood.

Phil was born there in 1918, on September 25, and a second son, Alfred, arrived two years later.

The Rizzuto youngsters went to P.S. 68 and lived the normal lives of growing-up city kids. The girls played with their dolls and such games as hop-scotch and rope-skipping while the boys played ball. Phil and his brother were at some game nearly all year round, baseball, softball, touch football or stickball in the streets. Even in the winter Phil would go out with Alfred or some other baseball-crazy youngster and have a "catch."

"They were always thinking of some kind of ball," Mrs. Rizzuto recalls. "Phil was the littlest boy in the games but he also was the fastest runner. I used to look out the window and see them playing touch football in the street, four or five to a side. He could run away from the bigger boys every time."

Some of the schools had baseball teams and played in the Public Schools Athletic League but P.S. 68 had none. So Phil learned to play ball on the sandlots—what few there were—and in the streets. His dad had given him a bat and glove when he was four, barely out of the toddling stage. Mrs. Rizzuto made Phil's first uniform when he was eight years old.

When he was 12, the family moved from Ridgewood to Glendale, Queens. Actually, the neighborhoods adjoin, though they are in different boroughs. Phil still hung out with his old pals and, at that time, made his debut in a big league ball park.

He was such a good player that he was able to play in company with boys three and four years older. He could hit and field and, as always, outrun everyone else. Rizzuto was an outfielder then and it was as a flychaser that he tried out for the neighborhood team—the Ridgewood Robins.

The coach was a man named Willenbucher and he was amused that the little kid should want a tryout. Willenbucher joshed him, not unkindly, when the tyke said he was an outfielder.

"I can see how you cover the outfield," he said. "You're a cricket!"

Phil, always a shy kid, grinned his embarrassment. The other boys, with the innate cruelty of children, called him "Shrimp," "Midget," "Runt" and "Little Dago."

But he bravely smiled at the taunts and, in the tryout, showed that he was a ballplayer. The Robins accepted him and he became the regular left fielder. Willenbucher entered the team in a sandlot tournament which was sponsored by a Brooklyn newspaper (now extinct), the *Standard Union*. Phil's team won in the eliminations and gained the final bracket, meeting the Coney Island Athletics for the sandlot championship of Brooklyn at Ebbets Field.

It would be story-book stuff to tell how Rizzuto won the big game with a hit but that would be a mile from the truth. His team won all right but the only ball the Scooter hit was a foul.

"I was only about four feet high," he recalls, "and I was playing left field. I felt lost out there in that great big outfield but I did catch a couple of flies and didn't make any errors. But, at bat, I wasn't supposed to do anything. Mr. Willenbucher wouldn't let me swing at all because he figured I'd get a walk every time up. I was so small they couldn't pitch to me. First I batted lefty, then switched to the other side. I

walked the first four times up but I took a swing the last time
—and fouled a ball which was so low that it flew up under
the mask of the umpire behind home plate and hit him on
the Adam's apple. He nearly choked and, boy, was he sore at
me!"

It is obvious that, from almost the very beginning of his
career, baseball's first switch-walker was a dangerous hitter!

Upon graduation from P.S. 68, Phil enrolled at Richmond
Hill High School, at the far end of Pop's trolley route. Occasionally, the little lad saved the nickel carfare by waiting
for the old man's car to come along. Every nickel counted,
back there in 1932, because those were the pre-New Deal times
when nearly every corner had a man standing on it—selling
apples.

Except for the athletics, Rizzuto didn't care too much for
school. Like many teen-agers, then as now, he considered the
classroom a necessary evil. A fellow had to study so as to pass
his grades in order to remain eligible for sports. He studied
just enough to pass and no more.

Phil was afraid he'd be laughed at because of his size, but
he answered the call for candidates anyway one Spring,
nominating himself as a left fielder.

Coach Al Kunitz, who formerly caught for Columbia
University, commented on Phil's size, but more kindly than
others had. "You'll never make it as an outfielder," he said,
after watching the youngster in practice. "But with a pair of
hands like you have and an arm like yours, what an infielder
you'll make. Rabbit Maranville was a midget but he became
a star."

Kunitz was right. Phil made the team as a third baseman
and he played well. After that first season of high school play,

Kunitz was sold on Rizzuto's ability to make the grade ultimately in professional baseball, despite his runty build.

Of course, high school competition wasn't enough and
Kunitz insisted that Phil get all the experience possible and
this meant amateur sandlot and semi-pro ball in the sum-
mertime. In his first two summers while in high school,
Phil played with the amateur Glendale Browns in a league
known as the Queens Alliance. In the summer of 1934, when
he was not yet 16, Phil moved up into better company. He
caught on with a light semi-pro club representing the town
of Floral Park.

That was the first team which paid him for playing. At
the end of the season, the players divided up what was left of
the admission charges after overhead was taken out. Each
player got $120 for playing in 80 games. Since the taking of
money would have affected his amateur standing and pre-
vented him from continuing his ball career at Richmond Hill
the following Spring, Phil played at Floral Park under an
assumed name, the fine Italian name of Reilly.

Phil resumed his high school ball playing the Spring of
1935 and was given an All-Scholastic rating, this time as a
shortstop. (He previously had been All-Scholastic at third
base.) Kunitz, with the persistence and endurance of an in-
surance salesman, tried to create opportunities for Phil. The
coach attempted to get him scholarships at both Fordham and
Columbia but Phil's grades were not good enough for admission to those colleges.

Phil was back in high school in 1936 but, as the gag goes,
he wasn't taking up anything but space. French and other
languages were throwing him and he was playing hookey too
often to keep up with his classmates. By mutual consent, Riz-

zuto and Richmond Hill High severed their connection in the Spring of that year.

Meanwhile, Kunitz wangled the Dodger and Giant try-outs for him. The coach also interested George Mack, a Yankee scout, in his little ballplayer and Phil was invited to a tryout at the fabulous Yankee Stadium.

Paul Krichell, head scout of the Yankees and the finest judge of baseball talent there is in the world, ran that tryout session. He didn't let Rizzuto's miniature build bother him. Paul, now 72, was smarter than the Giants and Dodgers had been. He gave Phil a real good look and liked what he saw. After a five-day tryout—five morning sessions of two hours apiece—Krich decided Rizzuto was worth a gamble.

He offered Phil a contract with Bassett, Virginia, of the Class D Bi-State League at a salary of $75 per month for the 1937 season. There was, of course, no bonus offered. That was before the days of the bonus-babies, who have grabbed off anywhere from $25,000 to a hundred grand in recent years. Rizzuto got nothing but the chance to become a Yankee.

Years later, Yank General Manager Ed Barrow said, "Rizzuto cost me fifteen cents, ten for postage and five for a cup of coffee we gave him the last day he worked out at the Stadium."

Never, but never, has fifteen cents gone so far.

Little Phil's minor league career was marred by a mishap at the start but then became as sensational as his recent years in the majors. Phil quickly became the most popular player on the 15-man squad, which was managed by Ray White, one-time Columbia University pitcher.

But one day Rizzuto injured his left thigh, developing a "charley horse"—the athlete's expression for a pulled muscle.

Usually such an ailment can be cured through rest. But Bassett had no extra infielders and Phil tried to keep playing. White massaged and bound the thigh before each game to ease the pain. But the treatment didn't cure the injury and, shortly before Memorial Day, White became alarmed and sent Phil to a Dr. Johnson for examination.

"What has happened," the doctor told him, "is that the muscle in your leg has pulled apart. It's something that happens maybe once in a million cases of strain."

Dr. Johnson said that an operation was necessary immediately, because gangrene had set in. Any further delay in cleaning out the infection would have been tragic for the tiny ball player. "If this had continued for a few more days, we would have had to take the leg off," the medic said grimly.

The timely and successful intervention of the surgeon's scalpel saved both the leg and Phil's career. After a couple of month's convalescence, he returned to the lineup and helped his team win the Bi-State pennant. He recaptured his speed on the bases and afield, too.

Krichell and George Weiss, director of the Yankees' farm system, digested glowing reports about Phil during the winter and decided to move the boy up to Norfolk of the Class B Piedmont League for the following season. There Phil joined second baseman Jerry Priddy and, together, they were to form the star keystone combination of the minors for three successive years.

Rizzuto and Priddy moved up to Kansas City of the American Association, one of the highest class minor leagues, for 1939 and continued to wow all onlookers. Little Phil whammed Association pitching for a .316 average.

The kids were ready for the big league but the Yankees

didn't need them. The big Bombers had won their fourth straight pennant in 1939 and didn't require replacements. So Jerry and Phil were kept at Kansas City for the 1940 season— and again they tore the league apart. Naturally, the Yankee front office had to advance the brilliant duo to the Yankee Stadium for the following season.

When they arrived in the St. Petersburg, Fla., training camp of the Yanks in February of 1941, Priddy and Rizzuto were marked men. Weiss had turned down an offer of $250,-000 by the Detroit Tigers for the pair. Everyone wondered whether or not they had the stuff. Rizzuto had one advantage which his sidekick lacked: There was a job waiting for Phil because shortstop Frankie Crosetti had faded the previous season, when the Yanks had finished third. Priddy had no opening because Joe Gordon was in his prime.

Both Priddy and Rizzuto got off badly at the start of the season in American League competition and had to be benched for a while. Crosetti took over short and Gordon, who had been switched to first base, returned to second. Phil succumbed to the pressure and excitement of the big league and batted only .200 for the first month of the season. Joe McCarthy wisely benched him for a month and then restored him to the lineup.

Once he returned to shortstop in June, Phil had the "feel" of things and was all right. He and Gordon teamed up to make stunning plays, day after day, for they were an agile, alert, reckless combination. The Scooter—he received that nickname from teammate Billy Hitchcock at Kansas City in 1939—was the perfect complement to Gordon.

Phil hit steadily, too, finishing up with a .307 average. His all-around talent helped restore the Yankees to the top of the league and earned him the honor as "Rookie of the Year."

The Dodgers won the National League pennant that year and the World Series, first ever between the Yanks and Brooks, was exciting. That was the series in which Mickey Owen's famed muff cost the Dodgers the fourth game and, ultimately, the series. For Phil, it wasn't a classic to remember, for he was not too happy with his performance. Actually, it was only at bat that he had failed—two grubby singles in 18 tries for an average of .111, with no runs scored and none batted in.

All in all, it had been a wonderful year for the little fellow—the Yankees, the pennant, the world championship. And then it was topped off, the very evening the Series ended, when he met *the girl.*

The Scooter's first "girl friend" was Betty Dresser, a brown-haired lovely he met in Kansas City in 1939. They were teen-age sweethearts, but it wasn't serious. That it might have become so, was possible. But tragedy struck the young lady. Betty underwent what seemed to be a simple tonsillectomy in 1940 and died from a post-operative throat infection.

There wasn't another lady in Phil's life until Joe DiMaggio failed to keep an appointment the evening of the final game of the '41 Series. The great center fielder was supposed to speak at the Fireman's Annual Smoker in the Essex House Hotel in Newark, N. J. He had to bow out in order to catch a plane for San Francisco that evening.

The Yankee Clipper asked little Phil to drive him to La-Guardia Airport in Queens and, en route, requested Phil phone Lt. Emil Esselborn, chairman of the affair, and express his regrets. Phil complied after leaving Joe at the airport and

Esselborn asked the shortstop if he would like to come as a pinch-hitter for Joe.

Phil did and made a hit with his speech. After the affair was over, Esselborn invited the little Yankee to his house for a cup of coffee. Phil went along and that turned out to be the most important cup of coffee of his life—even more so than the one Barrow had given him at Yankee Stadium. A step inside the front door of the Esselborn residence, the Scooter found his girl.

"The Kid," as he calls her, was ravishing, blonde Cora Esselborn, younger of the fireman's two daughters. The Dutch-Irish beauty, then nineteen, was a knockout. Today, the mother of three pretty little girls, she still retains her trim figure and probably is the most beautiful of the ball players' wives.

Phil began a whirlwind courtship, seeing Cora every day for a month. He asked her to marry him in November but she thought that was a bit soon. The young lady wanted to be sure. Pearl Harbor came a few weeks later and all thoughts of a marriage had to be postponed.

Phil and Cora saw each other infrequently during the '42 ball season, but they wrote when he was on the road and had an occasional date when the club was at home.

The draft board eventually reclassified him to 1-A and Phil decided he'd prefer the Navy to the Army. At that time, there was no draft for the Navy, which was still on a volunteer basis. In August, while the Yanks were winning the flag easily, Phil passed his physical and was able to have his actual induction delayed until after the World Series, which the Bombers dropped to the Cardinals in a big upset.

Rizzuto put away his bat and glove the day after the

Series ended and reported to Norfolk for "boot" training at the Naval Training Station. Phil wanted to get married at the end of the eight-week session but Cora had decided she would like to be a June bride. So the wedding was set for that month.

Phil and Cora were married at St. Mary's Church in Norfolk on June 23 and Cora took a small apartment in Norfolk to be near Phil. The idyll didn't last very long, however. The ball team was broken up by shipping orders which sent the players to overseas posts in December. Phil said a tearful goodbye to Cora, who had become pregnant, and sailed for Gammadodo, New Guinea, a few days after New Year's Day of 1944.

With the end of the war in August of '45, Phil and millions of others began to think of going home. He got out in September, by ship, and was en route to California while the Tigers were defeating the Cubs in the World Series.

The Scooter and the other famed Yankees, DiMag, Keller, Henrich, Gordon and Dickey returned to baseball the following Spring and the Bombers, naturally, were picked to win the pennant. Larry McPhail, who had taken over Barrow's post as general manager during the war, selected Panama as a training site for the Yanks and the team got into good shape in the tropical sun.

Unfortunately, the tropics didn't agree with Rizzuto. His malaria, contracted in the Pacific, recurred and he had to break his training grind. He lost weight and was weak. He recovered in time to start the regular season in April but was not himself. Nor were most of the others. The war had dulled the abilities of many of the great Yankees and there was a mass collapse. McCarthy failed to rally the team and was bounced by MacPhail May 24. Dickey took over but he failed to spark the club. The Red Sox won 40 of their first 50 games and ran off with the pennant.

When Phil cleaned out his locker at the Stadium in September, the little man wondered if he was doing so for the last time. Phil was afraid that he was washed up, even as Red Ruffing, Dickey, Atley Donald, Marius Russo, Ernie Bonham and Johnny Murphy. He was only 28 but there were signs that he was "through." Rizzuto, intelligent, sensitive, given to worrying, was well aware that his earning capacity seemed to be disappearing. And he had turned down the chance to grab many thousands of dollars by jumping to the Mexican League in April of that year.

Jorge Pasquel, president of the Mexican League, had made Phil one of the prime targets in his raids on the majors. He sent his brother Bernardo to woo Phil and Cora with thousand dollar bills, a Cadillac and an apartment in Mexico City. Phil, who was getting $7,500 from the Yankees, was offered a five-year contract at $12,000 per year and a ten-grand bonus to sign. He almost took it—and might have if Cora hadn't rejected the deal at the last minute. She decided that she didn't want to bring up her children in Mexico.

Phil's threat to leave the Yanks was known to MacPhail and the latter gave him a $5,000 bonus to remain in the American League.

Phil had to make good all over again in 1947, after his failure in the first post-war season. The shortstop came through, as did the others. In mid-July the Yanks tore off a nineteen-game winning streak which clinched the flag. Rizzuto's size five spike shoes were all over the infield and he performed in pre-war style. He erred only 25 times while handling 815 chances and, as manager Bucky Harris said, "He pulls a miracle out there each day. I wouldn't trade him for any shortstop in baseball. I don't care if he only hits .250, it's what he does with his glove, the way he saves our pitchers, that makes him great." Phil hit more than .250. He played in 153 games, missing only one, and whacked out a .273 average.

Rizzuto kept up the good work in the World Series, again against the Dodgers. Phil fielded perfectly, setting a Series record of putouts by a shortstop with 18 and he had 15 assists. He hit .304 and scored one run and drove in another as the Yanks took the seventh and deciding game, 5-2.

Off that fine performance, Rizzuto and the Yanks figured to cop the flag again in 1948. But everything went wrong. There was dissension between Harris and George Weiss, the general manager who had succeeded MacPhail following the Series victory in '47. Excepting that DiMaggio had a good season, it was 1946 all over again.

For Rizzuto, it was a brutal season and, once again, led him to wonder if he had lost his ability to stay in the big league. The Scooter was a walking ad for the band-aid manufacturers from start to finish. He pulled a muscle in his right thigh the first week of the season and was in and out of the lineup for a month. In June he began to suffer dizzy spells while chasing pop flies. In July his arm was affected and an X-ray showed bone chips in the vicinity of the elbow. It was his worst year. He batted only .252 and made only twenty-one extra base hits in 464 times at bat.

The Weiss-Harris Feud was dissolved the day after the 1948 season ended, with Bucky getting the boot although the club had been in the pennant race until two days before the finish.

Stengel became the new manager and he had his work cut out for him. One of his rehabilitation problems was Rizzuto. The old man let Phil run his own training program in St. Petersburg in the Spring, permitting the shortstop to baby his arm and legs. The idea worked well and Phil was in fine shape for the start of the season.

Although the club was beset by injuries—the total hit 73 by the end of the year—Phil missed only two games. He was, by any reasoning, the most valuable of all the Yankees. The little man led the club in the following offensive categories: games played, 153; at bat, 614; runs scored, 110; hits, 169; total bases, 220; stolen bases, 18; doubles, 22; and triples, 7. In addition, he led all shortstops in fielding with only 23 errors in 792 chances.

But Phil wasn't deemed the Most Valuable Player in the American League. That distinction went to Ted Williams, who had batted .343. The tall Red Socker received thirteen first place votes from the twenty-four man selection committee to Rizzuto's five.

Despite his brilliance, it just wasn't Phil's year to win elections. Although he had carried the team for the first half of the season while DiMaggio was recovering from heel surgery, the Scooter was ignored by the fans who voted for the All Star Game players. Eddie Joost, of the Philadelphia Athletics, and Vern Stephens of the Red Sox were named for the shortstop position.

After his tremendous work in '49 and the double rejection in both the All Star and MVP balloting, Rizzuto was downcast. He had enjoyed his greatest season and missed both nominations. He didn't figure to reach such a peak again and fully believed he'd never be in the running for the MVP award another season.

But he was wrong.

Phil began in 1950 with even a greater surge than he had shown in the previous season. With Henrich permanently lamed, for baseball purposes, DiMaggio in the worst batting slump of his career, and other veterans slowing down, a heavy load fell on Rizzuto's sturdy shoulders. The shortstop batted .355 in the first six weeks of the schedule and upped it to .441 as the Yanks swept all eight games on their first Western trip. At thirty-two, and in his tenth season, he was playing better than ever.

Rizzuto's fielding was even more startling than his batting. In fact, it was perfect. The Scooter didn't make an error until June 8 when he fumbled a roller by Bob Swift, Detroit catcher, in a night game in New York. That boot ended his errorless string at 288 chances in 58 games, a new record. He had committed his previous error—a bad throw—on Sept. 17, 1949.

There was no ignoring Phil in the All Star balloting this time and the mite was named American League shortstop for the first time. He played the entire fourteen innings as the National League won, 4-3.

Rizzuto never had a real slump all season and he wound up as fifth-best hitter in the league with a .324 batting average. As Henrich said one day, "This ball club can get along without me or anyone else—except one. We just keep praying that nothing happens to that little scamp at shortstop. He's the one we have to have every day."

It would have been a downright shame if Phil had missed getting the Most Valuable Player Award this time. He didn't, of course. The balloting wasn't even close, Phil being accorded 16 first place votes, with four going to Boston's Billy Goodman, the league batting champ, and three to Berra, the Yanks' catcher.

The MVP Award carries no cash with it, per se, but it serves the recipient as a bargaining weapon, second to none, at contract-signing time. Shortly after the World Series was over, George Weiss called Rizzuto into the Yankee offices on upper Fifth Avenue and signed him to a contract for $40,000— a raise of fifteen grand over his 1950 salary. So stout a pay boost is unusual and would not have been possible unless Phil had gained the Award, which is the highest individual attainment possible for a major leaguer.

For the third straight season the Yankees were involved in a tough pennant race in 1951 and they won it once more— with Rizzuto playing a key role. He slipped some from the heights of '50 but still was the best shortstop in the league and a highly valuable player for the Yanks. Again he played practically the whole season. In 1949 and '50 he had missed a total of three games. In '51, he was unable to play in only three—due to a bad leg—until the Yanks clinched the flag on the third-last day of the schedule.

The rest at the end of the schedule and the respite afforded by the three-day layoff as the Giants and Dodgers were playing off for the National pennant, aided Phil immensely. He was refreshed and ready when the World Series finally started and, for the first time in his career, actually starred in the series.

The Giants proved to be tough foes but the Yanks won their third straight world championship by taking four of six games. The Scooter was tremendous throughout. He set a record for shortstops in a Series with 40 chances accepted, but made one error—the famous one when Eddie Stanky booted the ball out of his hand on a steal of second and paved the way for a Giant win in the third game. And he took part in nine of the record number of ten double plays made by the Yankee infield. In the fourth game, which the Yanks won, 6-2, Rizzuto was in four double plays, highest by one player in a single Series game.

At bat, he was great, too. The little man slashed out eight hits in 25 times up for a .320 average, scored five runs, batted in three and stole three bases. One of his hits was a "Chinese" homer at the Polo Grounds, so-called because it was a cheap chip shot along the foul line which just did reach the right field stands—257 feet from home plate. That is the shortest possible homer in the majors and Phil earned the nickname "Ming Toy" for his "oriental fantasy."

The Scooter was a tired little guy in 1952, beset by stomach ulcers, yet he gamely stuck in there and managed to appear in all but two of the Yankee games. He retired to a hospital shortly after the conclusion of the victorious World Series against the Dodgers.

With the decline of DiMaggio and his decision to retire, little Phil has become the No. 1 Yankee, the man who must provide the personal brilliance and flaming inspiration in the years to come. Once the fans looked to Babe Ruth in right field to find the star in the Yankee Stadium scene; then to first base toward Lou Gehrig and after that out to center field where DiMag played. Now it's to the wide area between third and second bases and Phil Rizzuto, the greatest shortstop in the long, proud history of the New York Yankees!

CHAPTER IX

THE SURPRISE PACKAGE
(Gil McDougald)

BY BEN EPSTEIN

A United States Mail delivery truck braked to a halt in front of a San Francisco Post Office one afternoon in October of 1949. The driver, a tall, slender Scotch-Irishman, waved to William McDougald, talking to a Custom House co-worker on the steps of the building, and vaulted lightly to the sidewalk.

"Come here, son, before you knock off for the day," beckoned Mr. McDougald with a note of pride. "I want you to meet a friend of mine you should know.

"Shake hands with a fellow dispatcher. Gil, this is Mr. Coleman, father of Jerry Coleman of the New York Yankees. I'm sure he can give you a few helpful tips now you're also connected with the same baseball organization as is his boy."

Jerry's old man quickly sized up Gil's gangling six feet, two inches, 180 pounds of springy anatomy featuring a big pair of "infield" hands.

"You're certainly high and lean enough," appraised Mr.

Coleman, "the old-fashioned Yankee type. Just returned from the World Series where they took care of the Dodgers and I know what I'm talking about. Heard plenty about you from the local folks and it all adds up that you're going to be there right along with Jerry before long. You'll make it . . . just hang on there."

Gil recalled he sincerely thanked Mr. Coleman for the kind words but inwardly laughed off what he considered a conjecture even too ridiculous for a pipe dream.

"Whom did that nice old guy think he was kidding," thought young McDougald. "Me, a 20-year-old punk and a married one, at that, with a wife and kid to support. Imagine giving me a routine of making the Yankees just after I finished my second year of pro ball at Victoria in the Western International League, a Class B outfit. I'm still a truck driver, hauling letters around town in the off-season to guarantee the rent and groceries. And I recently learned I'd better start scouting around for some more Pablum since the family is gonna increase."

It's needless to recount, today, that those pessimistic reflections of Gilbert James McDougald boomeranged in two, swift meteoric years. So completely, in fact, that not even the prophetic Mr. Coleman could have conjured such a chain of successes. The repercussions of McDougald's runaway rise actually rattled through Mr. Coleman's household through the medium of Gil replacing the established Jerry at second base when he wasn't idling some other regular by operating at third.

The sudden whirl of McDougald's career following that conversational episode on the Federal Building approach spun a golf-stanced teen-ager from an "alien" sponsored amateur club in 1948 to the top as the American League's outstanding rookie in '51, and hitter of a Series grand-slam homer, the third in history.

McDougald still swings from that strange golfer-like position, although he has yet to adhere to a teammate's advice and holler, "fore," before facing the pitcher. He pulls the bat back on a level from the waist with the fat part of the wood, dipping down, assuring a flat swing propelling a rotary-action follow through.

A tourist, observing Gil's stance at the Yankees' Phoenix Spring training camp in '51, took one look and yelped, "Now, I've seen everything including a man swinging a bat below sea level!"

The Giants' Larry Jansen, who served Gil that momentous jackpotter in the fifth game of the last Series, doesn't think it's funny. Nor does Procopio Herrera, off whom he grand-slammed in St. Louis on May 3, 1951, to climax a record-tying six RBI (ninth) inning. The Yanks tornadoed across 11 in that frame to set a new scoring standard for the ninth.

McDougald research uncovers the fact that Gil kicked up his first grains of diamond dust, a minute pile, as a school-boy at San Francisco's Fairmont Grammar and Commerce High.

"Just write those down as two teams I made mostly in my imagination," grinned Gil. "I was just one of those who bounced around with the other kids in grade school. And as a freshman, sophomore and junior washout and a six-game second baseman as a senior in high school. Too skinny and brittle but I was a Joe DiMaggio in my own back yard. That's where I did the managin' and manufactured my swing, if you can call it that."

Gil started to "fatten up" at 18 and hooked up with the Bayside Braves, a school under the loose control of the Boston Braves. Bill Lawrence, a Braves scout, saw something in addition to—or in spite of—McDougald's pool-cue grip. Lawrence offered Gil a $500 bonus and $175 per month on a minor nine to be designated.

At the same time, a shrewd Yankee representative, the late Joe Devine, likewise detected Gil's peculiar plate posture and the identical clue of something gleaned by Lawrence. So Devine, familiar with the Yankee assets, blandly offered a $1,000 bonus and $200 per month. Without further bargaining (an exigency for which Devine was prepared, it was learned later) McDougald snapped up the proposition.

"It was no time to haggle," reviewed Gil. "I needed the dough and a thousand bucks looked like a million. Sure, I still was only a 19-year-old sandlotter, but also a married one; had been for several months and you'd be surprised how it makes one appreciate the value of a buck. I'd be lying, too, if I said getting a chance to become a Yankee didn't figure in persuading me to sign."

Once Yankee property, Mac got his orders to report to Twin Falls of the Class C Pioneer League in the campaign of '48. A second baseman, as he was at Fairmont, Commerce and Bayside, Gil clicked from the beginning. That is, until he fractured his right ankle in August. But the Yanks had seen enough to gratify. The kid hit .340.

They promoted Gil to Class B (Victoria) in '49, happily learned that the mended ankle didn't affect his speed, filed his name among the better prospects and patiently awaited results. It's a company policy to minimize advertisement concerning varsity fledglings, if at all possible. Still, the farm heads couldn't hide McDougald's .344 and his leading the Western International in doubles.

During the Winter of '49, Devine reported to the front office: "That Slim Jim of mine is good enough for Double A and, maybe, higher and I'll bet you a hat he'll hit .300 and hold his own in the field no matter in what league you assign him."

The Yankees decided on Class AA in '50, shipping Gil to Beaumont, their Texas League affiliate. The time had come to see if McDougald had it. Rogers Hornsby, who took over the Beaumont management after the death of Chick Autry, would give it to them straight. The great Rajah's ultimate stamp of approval even shocked Casey Stengel but that's getting ahead of the story.

"Playing under Hornsby was like being out on probation from reform school," sighed Gil, going over the Texas League phase of his development. "There's a gent who's really top kick when it comes to hewing to the line. I now can understand why he rates as the greatest right-hand hitter that ever lived.

"Believe me, Hornsby eats and sleeps baseball and then chews it up again. During the stretch drive for the pennant (won by Beaumont) he ordered us to cut out the movies, stop reading to save our eyes for the pitchers and even frowned at a hamburger if done too well. What made it rough was that he practiced what he preached."

Obviously, Mac stuck to the Hornsby regimen. He hit .336, drove in 115 runs in 557 times at bat. Texas League scribes voted him the circuit's Most Valuable Player, freak swing and all. Hornsby's lone comment on the swing, "It's a good one, it gets results. Stick to it and don't ever change."

A McDougald homer against the Athletics early in '51 elicited this keen analysis from Jimmy Dykes—"That flat swing is a phoney. It's the finish, not the beginning, that counts. And you see where they go when he finishes. As a player I knew the value of this swing but could never make it, which is why I don't ask my men to try it."

Likewise, it puzzled Stengel, Bill Dickey, Frank Crosetti, Tommy Henrich, DiMaggio, Johnny Mize, Yogi Berra, Phil Rizzuto and the rest of the veteran Yankees. It also intrigued Casey from a more selfish standpoint after he got a gander at Gil at Phoenix in the spring of 1951.

"That McDougald feller, who it says here, is on the Kansas City roster and who is supposed to be shipped to Lake Wales next week looks like a freak but he's lying—he's a big leaguer and I can prove it," said Stengel.

How Stengel planned to "prove it" stumped minds right up to General Manager George Weiss. Gil played second and second, only. His replacing the flashy and acrobatic Coleman, now a set star of two years, registered as preposterous. And Stengel's admitting it merely added to the confusion.

Casey's desire to experiment with McDougald stemmed from what he deemed an emergency, actually a personal secret. At that time, his third base two-platooning, in his opinion, lacked teeth. For the nonce, Dr. Robert Brown was interning at a San Francisco hospital and Billy Johnson remained in Augusta, Ga., a holdout.

While the left-hand-batting Brown commanded respect as a pretty good hitter against any kind of pitching and the right-hand-batting Johnson whacked an occasional long ball, Stengel liked neither as a third baseman. They, according to Casey, were too slow and were unable to go to both the right and the left.

Consequently, Stengel was secretly searching for a third baseman. Two days after McDougald was told his transportation had been arranged for the Kansas City squad's Florida camp, Casey ambled out to second base where Gil was one of a half-dozen working out. He singled out McDougald.

"Ever play third?"

"Never," replied a flustered Gil.

"Would you like to try?"

"Nope, that's not for me. I'd get lost over there."

"Well, move over there and try fielding and throwing a few. If you get lost, I'll call the police."

The very next day, Stengel called the road secretary instead of the cops. He ordered him to cancel McDougald's railroad ticket—indefinitely.

"Crosetti all but killed me hitting ground balls," Gil said as he reported the incident which definitely rushed him toward his big league opportunity and probably changed the entire course of his career. "Day after day, Frank let me have it. I like to field and throw but I also like to hit. My beef to Casey got this answer, 'You're all right as a hitter and you're improving as a fielder.' "

McDougald's unfolding as a potential star was further indicated when he held on after both Johnson and Brown slowed up. Gil also appeared in the daily camp stories with more frequency. The publicity soon put him on a par with those other standout rookies—Mickey Mantle and Tom Morgan.

Gil won his spurs in the Arizona and California exhibitions and, by the time the Yankees headed East, he already had been marked as the utility infielder, spelling Coleman at second when not handling third. Oddly, he looked more impressive at third, "out there, on the border," as he put it.

Seeing McDougald for the first time, Detroit's All-Star third sacker, George Kell, raved, "His action and hand movements are strictly star stuff and I believe I know a third baseman when I see one."

Nevertheless, Gil shifted on and off the spot during the first half of the '51 season. Mac was expendable for the simple reason that he could be farmed out. Which, of course, opened the door for a club squeezing down to the player limit without gambling on athletes vulnerable to the draft. And it might be inserted here, even the thought of losing the most inept goon for a paltry $10,000, shakes the Yankee empire.

Mac modestly admits he felt "pretty safe" up to the day before cutting down time. After all, he'd had his real big day in St. Louis with those six RBIs on a triple and homer in one inning. Also, he recalled reading somewhere where the White Sox had offered their slugging first baseman, Eddie Robinson, for him.

But on June 14, one day before the deadline, Stengel singled him out for another one of those charming chats. The dialogue, opened by Casey, double talk and all, went something like this:

"Got some bad news for you but it really ain't as bad as it sounds."

"When and where am I going?"

"Well, we may and may not send you to Kansas City but not because we don't want you if you understand what I mean."

140

"Will you repeat that?"

"Course, if a certain deal goes through before tomorrow midnight and they're willing to throw in another feller, you'll be all right—but maybe you'd better pack."

McDougald packed, then unpacked. The Yankees managed to waive Johnson out of the American League (nice slipping, if you can do it) and sold Billy to the St. Louis Cardinals.

Convinced that the Yankees wanted him, Gil slowly and surely matured as a valuable man on the club. He climbed to .300, wound up at .306, being the only regular to finish above the charmed circle. Mac was the first rookie to lead the club in hitting, the last being, ironically, the traded Johnson who did it with a comparatively smallish .280 in '43.

During the last 60 days, Gil operated either at second or third and, on a score of occasions, started at one and finished at the other. It's significant that on the day of his Series Slammer, Mac opened at second and finished at third. He carried the poise and know-how of a 10-year campaigner as indicated in Andy High's revealing "Yankee Book" (magnanimously turned over to the Giants):

"McDougald likes fast ball over the plate high. He is tough and can hurt you."

Naturally, McDougald rates his biggest thrill as his grand slammer (fast ball, over the plate high), off Jansen.

"You know how it is when you're lucky enough to do it in front of your old man who came all the way from San Francisco," he related. "It really worked like a charm because he kidded me after each of the first four games—'Well, when are you gonna hit one?' But I could never have done it had not Berra, DiMag and Mize loaded 'em up after two were out. I believe that Mize would have put one in the rightfield stands if Jansen had pitched to him.

"I suppose you heard how the quiz kid boys made a sucker out of me by asking if I knew who were the other two to hit series grandslams. I knew about Tony Lazzeri—everybody in San Francisco does—but, honestly, I never heard of that Elmer Smith. When somebody told me to say, 'some mug named Smith,' I figured he was kidding."

McDougald ranked "my No. 2 kick" as being voted the league's top rookie, barely beating out the White Sox's streaky Orestes Minoso. This caused Chicago's general manager, Frank Lane, to blow his top.

"That one really stirred up some smoke, didn't it?" grinned Gil. "I'm glad I won it but, personally, I believe the award should have gone to Minoso. He's lots of ball player, anywhere he works, can field and hit. There's nothing left."

Gil attributed the award all to luck as he did his large afternoon in St. Louis. He recalled that Jackie Jensen also tripled and homered in the same ninth inning. And fortune saw to it his triple scored two runs and his homer, four, while Jensen's triple scored only one and nobody was on when he homered.

McDougald tailed off badly in his sophomore year, dropping 40 points in his batting, yet he was employed every day in Casey's shuttle maneuvers between second and third. He hit another home run in the World Series, this time in his first time at bat in the opening game against the Dodgers.

Gil, who married a childhood sweetheart, the former Lucille Tochilin of San Francisco, now makes his home in the East, having purchased a house in Nutley, N.J. He has four children, the oldest of whom is just four.

The Surprise Package

As a result of his off-season proximity to the Yankee offices, McDougald does a great deal of winter work on the banquet circuit as an unofficial good-will ambassador for the club. He also acts as instructor at the American Baseball Academy, one of the greatest means yet devised of combatting juvenile delinquency.

With the emergence of Billy Martin as a dependable second baseman, Gil now spends most of his time at third, although he is ready to be switched to second if Stengel feels that Rizzuto should be rested and replaced by Martin at short.

CHAPTER X

THE GOLD DUST TWINS
(Hank Bauer—Gene Woodling)

BY TOM MEANY

In the spring of 1948, Larry MacPhail's two sons, **Lee and** Bill, were with the Yankees' Kansas City farm, even though their dad was no longer with the Yankee organization. On a visit to the St. Petersburg training camp of the Yanks the boys renewed acquaintance with many of the New York writers and pressed upon them an invitation to come over to the camp of the Blues at Lake Wales.

"We'll show you the man who's going to be the next Charley Keller for the Yanks," promised Lee.

"He hits a ball almost as hard as Charley right now," chimed in Bill.

"What's the name of this phee-nom?" asked one of the writers.

"Bauer, Hank Bauer," chorused the MacPhails. "He's going to be a star."

It was an enthusiastic description and, although Hank hasn't become another Charley Keller yet, there is still time.

With Gene Woodling he has paired to do a fairly effective job of filling the wide spot in left field made vacant by the fading of Keller.

The season the MacPhails plugged Bauer was not an especially good one for Kansas City, which finished sixth under the managership of Dick Bartell. Hank hit 23 home runs, batted in an even hundred runs and was called up to the Yanks in the waning weeks of the season but did nothing spectacular.

It was easy to see why anybody in the Yankee organization could see in Bauer the new Charley Keller. Big and rugged, Hank, who had four years of combat duty with the Marines in the Pacific, was once voted by his teammates as "the man most likely to succeed in a free-for-all." Called the Bruiser by his fellow players, Bauer is, like so many big guys, affable and amiable unless aroused. And few have shown any tendency to arouse him.

Bauer was on the Yankee roster when Casey Stengel took over the team in 1949 and he has been what might be termed a semi-regular ever since. Hank usually alternates with Woodling in left, although in Casey's two-platoon system he is likely to find himself anywhere.

The original plan was for the right-hand hitting Bauer to play left against southpaw pitching, while Woodling batted against the right handers. This, obviously, would give Gene more work than Hank because of the preponderance of right handers but somehow Bauer and Woodling have appeared in more than 100 games each in every one of their four seasons with the Yankees.

Bauer, although his lifetime batting average as a Yankee is .294, actually higher than that of Keller, still has a long way to go to become the new King Kong. For at least one game, however, the sixth game of the 1951 World Series, Bauer performed as sensationally as Keller ever did.

In this game Vic Raschi and Dave Koslo of the Giants were tied at 1-all going into the Yankee half of the sixth. With one out Yogi Berra singled and took second when Hank Tompson in right fumbled the ball. Joe DiMaggio drew an intentional pass and Bobby Thomson saved the day temporarily when he snagged Gil McDougald's screeching line drive. big Johnny Mize walked to fill the bases. Up came Bauer, whose batting average for the Series was an anemic .118. He whacked a solid drive far over Monte Irvin's head up against the railing of the stands in left and cleared the bases. At the time, it seemed like the blow that would win the Series for the Yanks, since it put them in front 4 to 1.

Bauer was the man of the hour, but he had to come through once more to maintain his laurels. The Giants, battling courageously, had made the score 4-3 in the ninth, with two out and a man on second. Sal Yvars, batting for Hank Tompson, slashed a vicious drive to right field. Bauer raced in for the sinking liner and slid feet foremost on his right side to pocket the ball for the final out and clinch the third straight World's Championship for the Yankees.

Although Bauer has all the qualifications to make him a star, he has not yet become one in the accepted sense of the word. He has exceptional speed of foot for a big man, a strong, accurate arm and he can hit for distance. He murders left-handed pitching and gives most types of right-handers trouble, too, with one notable exception. Side-arm right-handers bother him inordinately.

The popular story around the American League is that Bartell spotted this weakness when Bauer was playing for him at Kansas City and exposed Hank's Achilles heel to the rest of the league after he became a coach for Detroit.

This could be so but big league pitchers are pretty smart in their own right about spotting a weakness. I always remember the case of Luis Olmo, who was batting like a wild man for the Dodgers until one day in Pittsburgh when Xavier Rescigno, a Pirate right hander, suddenly side-armed him. It probably was the first time Luis had looked at that type of pitching and the expression on his face plainly showed that he fervently hoped it would be the last. The word sped around the league via the pitchers' grapevine. He was ruined for the year.

Olmo later came back to be a pretty fair hitter and there is a chance that Bauer can plug this chink in his armor. If he ever does—and he's only 30 as he opens the 1953 season— Bauer truly could be another Keller, extravagant as that claim sounded when it was first uttered by the MacPhail boys four years ago.

Leo Durocher, the first time he saw Bauer, declared that if he had his pick of all the young Yankees, Hank would be his choice. Another astute judge of baseball talent who was smitten by Bauer at first sight was Clark Griffith, the Old Fox of the Senators. Hank played with Kansas City in a Florida exhibition game against Washington in 1947 and Griffith promptly offered half his ball club for him.

Although Stengel's two-platooners have won four straight pennants for him, none of them cottons to the idea of being a part-time ball player, least of all Bauer. He probably is the most fretful Yankee on the roster when he is on the bench. He wants to play every day—and he doesn't mind letting Casey know it, either.

A product of East St. Louis, Illinois, home of so many

good ball players, Bauer started out with Oshkosh, Wisconsin, where he tried several skills, including pitching. Hank picked Oshkosh because his brother had been a catcher there but after the 1941 season, Bauer enlisted in the Marines and was made a free agent when he returned in 1946, the Wisconsin State League having suspended operations during the war.

Frank Lane, now general manager of the White Sox, was the man responsible for bringing Bauer into the Yankee organization, a fact he now probably regrets. Frank, as business manager at Kansas City, signed Hank for a bonus of $250 and assigned him to Quincy, Illinois, in the Three-Eye League with instructions that he concentrate on the outfield.

In his brief career, Hank spent more time with the Marines than he did with any single ball club and his leatherneck roots are still deep. When the Yanks played a series of exhibitions in California in the spring of 1951, Bauer was met by squads of his old buddies at almost every stop. When the team played at San Francisco, Hank spent most of his time at the Marine barracks there.

Hank feels he owes a lot to the Marines. It was because of his affiliation with them that he met his charming wife. When Bauer was playing with the Blues, a couple of his Marine friends looked him up while passing through Kansas City. He went into the club's offices to request a couple of passes for his pals and thus met Miss Charlene Friede, the club secretary. It was love at first sight and the pair were married after the 1949 World Series.

Unlike Bauer, Woodling is not a product of the Yankee farm system. It was by a devious route that Gene wound up in Yankee Stadium. His path included major league stops, although somewhat brief ones, at Cleveland and Pittsburgh, as well as stretches at such widely separated points as Mansfield, Ohio, Newark and San Francisco.

Born in Akron, Ohio, on August 16, 1922, Gene is about two weeks younger than the man he has been sharing left field with, Bauer. Woodling was picked up by Cleveland scouts and shipped to Mansfield in the Class D Ohio State League in 1940. He proved he wasn't a bad pick-up by hitting at an awesome .398 to lead the league in batting, a stunt he was to repeat in three other leagues. Gene led the Michigan State League the next year when he batted .394 for Flint and the Eastern League in 1943 with .344 at Wilkes-Barre. He topped the Pacific Coast League in 1948 with .385 at San Francisco.

Woodling, like Bauer, feels that he hasn't yet reached his full potentialities as a Yankee. Gene thinks that the right field barrier at the Stadium is made to order for him but it wasn't until 1951 that he began to get the range. He hit 15 homers in '51, contrasted with a grand total of 11 in his previous two seasons with the Yanks.

An exceptional outfielder, who can play center as well as left, Woodling has made some remarkable catches for the Yankees, yet the fielding play he is most often asked about was a simple error of the common or garden variety, an ordinary fly he muffed in the fourth and final game of the 1950 World Series with the Phils.

Eddie Ford, the brilliant freshman left hander of the Yankees, had the Phillies shut out on four scattered hits as he went into the ninth with a 5-0 lead. The Phils had men on first and third with two out when Andy Seminick wafted a fly to Woodling. Gene got under the ball after a short run and dropped it, permitting two runs to come in. When Mike Goliat followed with a single, Stengel lifted Ford and sent in Allie Reynolds to preserve the victory, which the Chief did by fanning pinch-hitter Stan Lopata on four pitches.

"I still can't tell you how I came to muff that ball," declares Gene. And, considering that in the course of the 1950 season he had handled nearly 300 chances with only two errors, nobody else can determine how Woodling missed the ball, either. He doesn't miss very many.

When Woodling hit his first World Series home run against Sheldon Jones of the Giants in 1951, his average was only .167. But ordinarily, Gene is a dangerous batter in Series play; he batted over .400 against the Dodgers in 1949 and the Phils in 1950.

One of Woodling's most valuable assets as a Yankee is that, like Eddie Lopat, he is poison to Cleveland, the club which gave him his start. Gene always hits better against the Indians than any other club and he caused a sensation in their home city in 1951 when he claimed there was a spy planted in the scoreboard using binoculars to steal the Yankees' signals.

"No sign stealer is going to beat me out of my World Series share," proclaimed Woodling. He couldn't prove his case but insisted that this particular, and peculiar, form of espionage in Cleveland's Municipal Stadium dated back to when he played with the club in 1946.

There are some who believe Woodling's one-man vendetta against the Indians goes back to his association with them when he felt, perhaps, that he didn't get a fair chance to prove his worth. It could be that the fact he comes from nearby Akron serves as a spur to him whenever he plays against Cleveland.

Woodling was batting a measly .188 with Cleveland in

1946 after he returned from service and was traded to Pittsburgh for Al Lopez, currently the resident genius at the Tribal Tepee. Gene didn't do a great deal better with the Pirates in 1947 and was sent to Newark, where he came into the Yankee chain. His season at San Francisco in 1948 kept him with the Yanks and he had no greater booster than Stengel. Casey, who won the pennant that year with Oakland in the Coast League, had plenty of opportunity to appraise Gene's worth.

Expressing his feelings about Cleveland, Gene delivered a blow in 1951 which will remain in his memory book for a long time. He broke up a scoreless pitching duel between Bobby Feller and Reynolds with a seventh-inning homer and Reynolds made the picture complete by pitching a no-hitter!

Woodling had his best season as a Yankee in 1952, hitting .309 and topping it off with a smashing .348 against the Dodgers in the World Series. He hit safely in six of the seven games, including a pinch-triple in the opener and a home run in the seventh game.

Meanwhile Bauer edged a little nearer his self-set goal of 20 home runs by collecting 17, the most he ever hit in one season as a Yankee. His average was a respectable .293, twelfth among the American League regulars.

CHAPTER XI

YOUNG DOCTOR BROWN
(Bobby Brown)

BY TOM MEANY

It was an exotic trip the Yankees had in the spring of 1946, not the least unusual feature of it being that they trained in the Canal Zone. It was the first year of post-war training and the war-time fill-ins were looking somewhat awedly at men like Joe DiMaggio, Charley Keller, Tommy Henrich, Joe Gordon, Phil Rizzuto, Bill Dickey and others back from the services. There were, in fact, so many ball players around that when the squad returned from Panama, the Yankees had two bases in Florida, one in St. Petersburg for the regulars and one in Bradenton for the "B" squad.

When President Larry MacPhail called a press conference in St. Pete none of the assembled scribes guessed that its purpose was to announce that the Yanks were acquiring another player. There already were enough players around to win a couple of pennants. Or so it seemed.

MacPhail explained that the newest Yankee was an unusual young man. Just turned 21, he was the greatest shortstop in the history of the game and he had received the greatest bonus ever paid an amateur. He was studying to be a doctor and he had spent 30 months in the Navy.

The boy's name, explained Larry, was Bobby Brown. He had been trained to be a ball player since his infancy by his dad and there was nothing he couldn't do, just nothing.

MacPhail went on at a great rate, possibly to justify the bonus, said to be between $30,000 and $50,000; indeed a record for that time. He painted a picture of the young man so glowing that he seemed to be a combination of Hans Wagner and Lou Boudreau, with faint overtones of Superman. The writers began to get a little bored. Finally the late Will Wedge decided to ask a question.

"Larry," asked Will, "do you think Rizzuto will finish out the week at short?"

That broke up the press conference.

A day or two later the writers got their first look at Brown, a personable young man indeed. Tall, lithe, fair-complexioned, Bobby proved to have poise beyond his years, a natural intelligence and innate courtesy. Nobody who met him could help liking him. As a person, that is. On the ball field, the scribes still had to be shown.

Brown, quickly named Golden Boy by the writers because of his complexion, his bonus and his build-up by MacPhail, made a good impression at the plate. He stood up straight, well back in the box, choking the bat slightly. He had a good eye for the ball, both for following it and ignoring bad pitches. A left-handed batter, he wasn't noticeably embarrassed by southpaws.

At short, however, Brown seemed a little stiff in his motions, a little slow in breaking on ground balls. He certainly wasn't going to take Rizzuto's job that week. Or that year. When one of the writers had the temerity to suggest to Mac-Phail that Brown didn't seem too agile at short, Larry was outraged.

"Wait and see," growled the Yankee boss.

Brown was shipped to the Newark farm and all he did there was bat .341 and lead the International League in base hits with 174. When the figures were released, MacPhail sought out the writer who had been the Florida doubting Thomas when Golden Boy was first unveiled.

"What do you think of Brown, now?" challenged Mac-Phail. "I hope you noticed he led the International League in base hits."

"Yes," answered the writer, "and I also notice that he led all the shortstops in errors."

Brown came to the Yanks at the tag-end of the '46 season, appeared in seven games as a shortstop and third baseman, batted .333 and made *no* errors!

In the winter of 1946-47, MacPhail announced more than once that Brown would get a trial as a first baseman in spring training. Larry was dissatisfied with the incumbent, Nick Etten, and he wanted to get Brownie into the daily lineup. Through a strange twist of circumstances, Brown and Etten roomed together one night in February, 1947, at the Hotel New Yorker before the squad enplaned on its hop to Puerto Rico.

"I searched the kid's bags when he left the room," confided Etten to a friend at dinner, "and he had no first baseman's mitt. If he had, I'd have thrown it out the window."

Brown wasn't to be the Yankee first baseman that year—nor was Etten, as a matter of fact. (It turned out to be George McQuinn.) Bucky Harris tried Bobby at short, but he couldn't move out Rizzuto, nor could he chase the dependable Billy Johnson from third. Bobby nevertheless got in almost half of the Yankee games and batted an even .300.

It was in the World Series that Golden Boy paid off for MacPhail. Facing Brooklyn in a knockdown and drag-out, seven-game affair, Brown was merely terrific. Used only as a pinch-hitter, Bobby made World Series history with an average of 1.000!

In the first game, Brown batted for Frank Shea in the fifth inning with the bases filled and walked, forcing in a run and getting credit for an R.B.I. Not only that, but it took two pitchers to walk him, Ralph Branca and Hank Behrman, who relieved Branca.

Brown wasn't heard from again until the sixth inning of the third game when he appeared as a pinch-hitter for Spud Chandler and tagged Branca for a double, which led to a two-run inning for the Yanks. Bobby then rested until the sixth game when he appeared as a pinch-hitter for Jack Phillips and singled home a run, again against Branca.

In the seventh game, this time against Hal Gregg, Brown batted for Bill Bevens and whacked out a double to drive in another run. In four trips against Brooklyn pitching, Golden Boy had drawn one pass, hit one single and two doubles, scored twice and batted in three runs!

This was the beginning of a great World Series record for Bobby. The Yanks weren't in the Series in 1948 but against Brooklyn again in 1949, Brown, playing third regularly in the last three games of the five-game set, wound up with a .500 average and five runs batted in, the high for the Series. One of his belts in this series was a triple with the bases filled.

In the four game sweep over the Phillies in 1950, Bobby

batted .333 and against the Giants in 1951 he had an average of .357. His lifetime average for World Series play is a cool .439. Maybe MacPhail wasn't talking so extravagantly that day in St. Pete after all.

Bert Dunne, in his marvelous technical baseball book *Play Ball!* (Doubleday & Co., 1947) cites Brown as proof positive that ball players can be made as well as born. After five years in the major leagues, the indications are Bert should qualify his statement. Hitters can be made, not ball players.

Brown is by no means a poor fielder but he isn't a good enough one to get by with his glove alone. Bill Brown, Bobby's dad, had his heart set on making a big leaguer of the boy when he was no older than nine. He worked constantly with him and worked intelligently. He taught Bob to hit but there was no way he could teach him the art of breaking to one side or another. Undoubtedly the instructions Brown had from his dad improved his fielding but he still is stiff and angular when he plays a ground ball.

Bob's father hung a baseball from the ceiling in the cellar of the Brown home, gave Bobby a bat and started the curriculum. Mr. Brown decided that his son would have more chance as a left-handed hitter and started him that way, swinging at the moving ball, which became a low pitch or a high pitch by lengthening or shortening the string.

It was the senior Brown who taught Bobby to hit from the back of the box—as Rogers Hornsby did—so that he would have that much more time to sight the delivery. He educated Bobby to the level swing, to the principle of meeting the ball and following through. Although Bobby's average has tapered off from the .300 he hit his first two seasons with the Yanks—

and there are reasons for that which will be discussed later—he has one of the most remarkable batting eyes in the majors. He can punch hits to either field like one of the Waners, although not as often.

Perhaps Bobby would have been the perfect ball player his father dreamed of had it not been for his interest in medicine. After the family moved from New Jersey to California, Bobby certainly looked the part at Galileo High in San Francisco (Joe DiMaggio's alma mater) with various American Legion and semi-pro teams of the Bay area. When it came time to enter college, Bobby chose Stanford. He entered as a pre-med student and he also enrolled in the Naval Reserve, for this was in 1941.

When the Navy called Brown up he continued with his medical studies at Stanford, played college ball there in his freshman year. He was shifted around a great deal by the Navy, but always as a medical student. He went to UCLA and then to Tulane.

Brown desired every bit as much to be a doctor as he did a major leaguer, maybe more. He played ball when he could but he hit the books like a regular grind. Bobby knew that if he became a professional ball player—and he didn't doubt his ability to make it—his study time would be cut in half and it would take him twice as long to get his MD.

It could be that Brown might have made it all the way as a ball player, fielding as well as batting, if his studies hadn't come first. Most of the big leaguers of today put in six or more consecutive months of baseball annually while in their 'teens. Brown couldn't.

Bobby, self-effacing and modest, can't be lured into talking about himself but some who feel they know him well believe that Bobby, after the first romance of baseball had worn off, was lured more and more by the dream of being a surgeon. When the Yanks had Dr. Marvin A. (Mal) Stevens as their physician on their Caribbean tour in 1947, Bobby spent a great deal of time with Mal and it wasn't baseball they were talking.

It is hard to read another person's mind, unless you're Dunninger and that's your racket, but it is my opinion that Brown has stayed in baseball only because he is a conscientious young man. He felt that he owed it to his dad to make good—and certainly his father must have been proud at Bobby's World Series exploits—and he felt, too, that he was in debt to the Yankees for the bonus he received when he signed.

Brown, frequently a late arrival at training camp because of his medical studies, was in far-off Korea when the Yankees assembled for training in St. Petersburg in 1953. He was called up by the Army as a doctor during the All-Star intermission in July of 1952. He appeared only briefly with the Yankees before that. Bobby forsook single bliss shortly after the '51 season ended. It is unlikely that he will return to baseball.

Young Dr. Brown was unique among the Yankees. In the midst of a successful baseball career, he still had his future assured in another profession. Studious, quiet and abstemious, Brownie managed to be a part of the Yankees nonetheless. He was respected by his teammates, popular with the fans and an extremely dangerous clutch hitter. Brown, senior, did a good job of manufacturing a ball player.

Bobby finally settled down as the Yankee third baseman—as much as anybody can settle down in the Yanks' two-platoon system. He shared third with Billy Johnson when the Bull was still a Yankee and in 1951 he shared it with Gil McDougald.

Young Doctor Brown

He had never been a regular in the true sense of the word since he came to the Yanks, yet he was still an important member of the ball club.

Whether Brown would have blossomed into a star of the first water had his baseball work not been interrupted by the war or if he had been allowed to play regularly is a question which never will be answered. All you can go by is the record in baseball and on the record you have to see Golden Boy as a dangerous hitter—no more, no less. If that sounds critical, figure out how many dangerous hitters there are in baseball.

CHAPTER XII

THE KID
(Mickey Mantle)

BY TOM MEANY

Tom Greenwade is a hunter by instinct, avocation and profession. It is his pleasure to flush quail and other small game in the hills of his native Ozarks and his business to beat the bushes for young ball players wherever they may be found. He believes that he found one of the very best virtually on his own doorstep, which didn't come as a complete surprise to Tom, since he once came home from a day in the woods to find Harry S. Truman in his own kitchen.

Greenwade is a Nimrod of such repute around his home in Willard, Missouri, that it seemed only natural that Mr. Truman, in his pre-Presidential days, should pop over from Independence to seek Tom's assistance in arranging a hunting trip. But in some circles, potential big-leaguers are considered harder to come by than future Presidents, and Greenwade would sooner talk of bagging outfielder Mickey Charles Mantle, the twenty-year-old Yankee property, than of going a-hunting with Harry.

It seems safe to say that no rookie ever started a season in the big time with so little public notice and such enthusiastic professional fanfare as Mantle did in 1951. Joe DiMaggio had established himself as a star in the Pacific Coast League before he ever wore a Yankee uniform, and the bugles that blew for Clint Hartung when he came out of the Army to join the Giants were sounded by nonprofessionals. It was the ballplayers themselves who beat the drums for young Mickey—the World Champion Yankees and the members of such teams as they played in their extensive spring barnstorming tour.

Mantle came to the Yanks' Phoenix training camp in 1951 as a shortstop from the Joplin, Missouri, club of the Class C Western Association. He was not even on the Yankee roster, but was attached to their American Association farm at Kansas City. By opening day, he was in right field in Yankee Stadium, playing alongside DiMaggio, before more paid admissions than he had seen in his entire first season in organized ball, 1949.

If the jump Mantle made was a prodigious one, the pressure he was under was equally great. He had no more than 20 games to his credit in the outfield when he opened the season with the Yankees. As Casey Stengel, who has won pennants with the Yanks four years hand running, expressed it: "The kid is jumping five classifications at once and is going into a strange position. If he can make it, he's a wonder."

Mantle ran into a slump in the first series against the Athletics, being blanked in two straight games, although it took an acrobatic catch by Emil Valo near the Stadium's left-field bull pen to deprive Mickey of his first major-league homer.

When the Yanks opened in Boston, Stengel benched Man-

161

tle, explaining that the wide territory in right field in Boston, plus the sun and the wind made it a tough field to cover.

"I don't want to put any additional pressure on the boy," said Casey. "He never wore sunglasses until a couple of weeks ago. In my opinion, he's a big-leaguer right now but he has the handicap of having to learn a new position."

The cumulative pressure of Mantle's nineteen years and the heat of the 1951 American League race forced Stengel to option Mickey out in mid-July. The kid was sent to Kansas City on a 24-hour recall. With the Blues, Mickey was to be used in center field, the idea being to groom him to succeed DiMaggio. After a slow start, Mantle went on a home run binge which was the sensation of the American Association and he was soon recalled.

Mantle provided one of the strange thrills of the World Series when he collapsed in right field in the fifth inning of the second game. Willie Mays raised a high lofting fly to right-center. Both DiMaggio and Mickey went for the ball and suddenly Mantle fell prostrate to the turf. Joe made the catch and then hastened to where Mantle lay motionless. There wasn't a sound from 66,018 fans as DiMag bent over the kid. Finally Joe waved for the stretcher-bearers. Mickey's knee had given out under him. His reason for lying motionless was a fear that he had broken his leg.

The knee responded to treatment during the winter and Mickey, with a season under his belt, expected to be a regular with the Yanks. His freshman year wasn't bad for a boy making the jump from Class C. He appeared in nearly 100 games, batted .267 (four points higher than DiMag) and hit 13 home runs, some of them really long clouts.

Before the 1951 training season, almost nobody expected

The Kid

to see Mantle start for the Yankees. Even when he was knocking down fences in Arizona and California in the spring, it was assumed he would be sent to Kansas City for a year's schooling. That was the way General Manager George Weiss figured it, and Manager Stengel agreed with him. But Mantle's .402 batting average in spring training, against pitchers ranging from collegians to big-leaguers, simply couldn't be denied.

In the final exhibition game of the spring, against the Dodgers at Ebbets Field, young Mickey made three singles and a home run, the latter clearing the 38-foot scoreboard at a point 344 feet from the plate. The Sunday night before the season was due to open, he signed a Yankee contract, sitting in a drawing room with co-owners Dan Topping and Del Webb on the train taking the champs to Washington. (It called for about $7,500 for the season.) The game with the Senators was rained out, but in the opening series against the Red Sox, Mickey batted .333 and knocked in runs with each of his hits.

The story of Mantle the ballplayer goes back a long way—a couple of generations, in fact. It goes back to his late grandfather, Charley Mantle, who was a left-handed pitcher for an Oklahoma lead-and-zinc mining company and an incurable baseball fan. His son, Elvin, inherited the baseball mania, pitched for the same company team, and passed the bug along to his son.

When Elvin Mantle looked on his first-born he was determined that the child should be a professional ballplayer, a status neither he nor his dad ever had achieved. With that thought in mind, the infant was christened Mickey Charles Mantle—the Mickey after catcher Mickey Cochrane, then in his heyday with Connie Mack's Athletics.

As soon as young Mickey was able to wield a bat, his

163

father and his grandfather took turns pitching to him, the grandfather left-handed, the father right-handed. Mickey was taught to bat right-handed against his grandfather, left-handed against his dad, which is the origin of the youngster's success at the almost forgotten art of switch hitting.

Mantle is the most powerful switch-hitter the game has known. In an exhibition in Pittsburgh in 1953, he hit a home run left-handed where only two ever had been hit and later right-handed he hit one 565 feet in Washington.

Mantle is a bigger boy than he looks. His 175 pounds are solidly distributed and he stands five feet 10 inches tall, although he seems shorter because of his broad shoulders. Mickey's arms are well muscled but not knotted, and he has the forearms of a heavyweight boxer. During spring training, the other Yanks would kid him about the way his back muscles rippled when he leaned over to tie his shoes.

Mantle has been declared physically ineligible for the Army because of chronic osteomyelitis, a bone inflammation of the left foot that resulted from an accidental kick when he was playing football in the backfield of the Commerce, Oklahoma, High School. The case is arrested at present and it doesn't affect Mickey's speed, although double-headers sometimes tire him. He was put in 4F in his original draft examination and then re-examined twice in 1951 by physicians at the Miami, Oklahoma, Selective Service board and again classified 4F.

Mickey was born in Spavinaw, Oklahoma, on October 20, 1931. While he was still an infant, the family moved some 45 miles northeast to Commerce. It was here, hard by one of the "chat" piles—pebbly refuse mounds common to that lead-and-zinc mining country—that his grandfather and father gave him his first baseball lessons.

Until he became Yankee property, all of young Mantle's life revolved around the northeast corner of Oklahoma, the southeast corner of Kansas and the southwest corner of Missouri. It was at Commerce High that he played baseball and football under coach John Lingo and it was at Baxter Springs, Kansas, that Mickey was playing when Scout Greenwade signed him.

"I first heard of Mickey when he was in his third year at Commerce High in 1948," recalled Greenwade. "A fellow named Kenny Jacobson, who was in the Commerce Fire Department and who served as an umpire in the Ban Johnson League, a loop about one step ahead of American Legion baseball, told me about him.

"I went over to see him play at Alba, Missouri, but I wasn't particularly impressed. The boy was only sixteen then and hadn't his full growth. They used to call him 'Little Mickey Mantle' in those days. I couldn't have signed him anyway, because he was still in school, but Kenny kept giving me reports on the boy. Finally, in his last year, I saw him with Baxter Springs in the Ban Johnson League.

"Mickey got his high-school diploma on a Friday night and Sunday I saw him play a game in Coffeyville, Kansas, Walter Johnson's home town. Just as the game ended in the ninth, there was a terrific rainstorm. Mickey, his dad and myself ducked into my car behind the grandstand and that's where he was signed."

Mantle was then taken to a Yankee tryout camp at Branson, Missouri, where he worked out for a few days before being sent to Independence in the Kansas-Oklahoma-Missouri League. Mickey was no fabulous bonus baby. He received, roughly, $1,100 for signing, a far cry from the $100,000 the Pirates paid Paul Pettit.

"I disremember what the exact amount was," grinned Greenwade, "but I know we figured out what Mickey's salary would be for the remainder of the season with Independence and it came to around $400. To avoid the bonus rule then in effect, a boy signed to a Class D contract couldn't receive more than $1,500 for bonus and salary in his first year, and we were mighty careful to keep it under that. A dollar or two more would have put him in the bonus class."

Cappy Stewart, business manager of Independence, still has the canceled check, suitably framed. Because, like Greenwade, Stewart had been quick to appreciate the historical implications of Mantle's first contract.

Playing the balance of the 1949 season at short for Independence, Mantle hit a modest .313 against the Class D pitchers of the K-O-M League—four points below the league's leading hitter. Managed by Harry Craft, Independence won the pennant and the play-offs. In 1950 both Craft and Mantle were promoted to Joplin in the Western Association and again their team won the pennant. By now, Mickey was really cutting loose at the plate. He led the league with an average of .383 and hit 26 home runs, 14 left-handed and a dozen right-handed.

Although Mantle burst like a bombshell on the writers in 1951, it can't be said he came as a surprise to the Yankee brass, which realized all along it had something special in the switch hitter from Oklahoma. In 1950, Stengel and the coaching staff conducted a baseball seminar at Phoenix in advance of spring training and young Mr. Mantle was one of the prize pupils. Baseball Commissioner Happy Chandler ordered the school disbanded, since it jumped the gun on the March 1st training inaugural; but while classes lasted, Mickey was a sensation.

"I was pitching batting practice when the kid came to the plate," recalled Bill Dickey, Yankee coach. "The boy hit the first six balls nearly 500 feet, over the lights and out of sight. He hit them over the fences right-handed and left-handed and he hit 'em over the right-field fence right-handed and the left-field fence left-handed.

"When Mantle was playing short he didn't impress me as being particularly fast, but when we divided the boys up for a series of 75-yard sprints, Mickey finished first in his group, looking over his shoulder at the others. Then we had a sprint for the winners and he won that, too. Then he got sick and explained that he wasn't in shape!

"I honestly believe Mantle is the fastest man I've ever seen in a baseball uniform. I always picked Ben Chapman (the old Yankee outfielder) as the fastest, but I think Mickey could have outrun Ben."

Brief as was Mantle's stay in the school in Phoenix in February, 1950, it convinced Greenwade that he had come up with a true gem amid the lead-and-zinc mines of Oklahoma. Later that spring, in the Florida camp of the Yanks at St. Petersburg, Tom told some of his friends among the newspapermen that he thought he had a star in the making.

"Greenwade felt that way all through 1950," related the late Hank DeBerry, onetime battery mate of Dazzy Vance who then scouted for the Giants. "That November he and I were at the same hotel in Caracas, Venezuela, for the Pan-American games and Tom kept telling me he felt he finally had come up with a kid who couldn't miss."

What Stengel saw in Phoenix was enough to give him

ideas about Mantle, too. After Joplin had won the 1950 Western Association pennant, Mickey was called East to work out with the Yankees. By that time, the Yanks were up to their ears in a pennant battle and nobody had too much time for the kid. He got in a lick or two in batting practice, worked at shortstop in infield practice, and took the last Western trip with the club.

"In actual playing experience, it probably meant nothing to the kid," explained Casey, "but it got him used to being around big-league ball parks. It let him get the feel of being with the Yankees."

That experience, brief as it was, may have stood Mantle in good stead. When he opened the 1951 season as a Yankee, he wasn't fresh—but he wasn't shy either. He talked politely, if not volubly, to reporters, posed for photographers willingly, even when they insisted on posing him with DiMaggio. The Clipper is the kid's idol and in the early days of spring training Mickey acted as though it were something of a sacrilege to have Joe dragged into a picture with him.

One newsman approached Mantle in late April and referred to a conversation Mickey had had a couple of days before with another writer. The youngster looked puzzled.

"Maybe I talked to him," he said. "But I've talked to so many writers since the team returned to New York that I really can't tell one from the other."

Mantle's confusion is understandable. When he was in Oklahoma for his draft examination, Greenwade, his discoverer, gave him the names of several newspapermen friends and suggested that he look them up.

"I forgot entirely the names he'd told me," confessed Mantle later. "I'm not used to talking to writers. I try to be obliging, although I'd much sooner be in the outfield practicing, which is what I really need."

Mantle is blond-haired, with a close trim which isn't far removed from a crew cut. He has blue eyes, a fair complexion and a skin that hasn't had too many hassels with a razor.

In batting, Mickey uses a modified spread stance of perhaps 24 inches and a stride of about six inches. He grips the bat at the end, holding his arms away from his body and indulges in a minimum of nervous bat-waggling. When the pitcher is ready to pitch, Mickey is ready to hit.

Making Mantle over into an outfielder early in 1951 was a major task and the kid acquitted himself amazingly well. Old Reliable Tommy Henrich, then a Yankee coach, had the job of schooling Mickey in the pregame drills. When play started, DiMaggio took over. By shouted directions, Joe moved Mantle into position for the various batters, and when the kid started after a ball, DiMag kept "talking" him into the catch. As Joe shifted to his left or right, the rookie shifted with him, and when a ball was hit into Mantle's territory, DiMag stayed within shouting distance.

On high flies hit to right center, Joe occasionally allowed Mickey to make the catch, even though he could have taken the ball himself. This, Joe felt, would build up Mantle's confidence.

"I can appreciate what he's going through," said the Clipper. "I had played before large crowds in the Coast League before I came to the Yankees, but I was still shy and afraid to talk, for fear I'd say the wrong thing and make a clown of myself."

DiMaggio has come a long way since those days, and his quotes on Mantle are to the point. "The boy has power on either side, and great speed. The longer he plays, the better he'll be able to stand off the pressure."

After the opening game in 1951 against the Red Sox, Stengel asked Mickey how he had felt in the outfield. "All right, I guess," Mantle replied, "but Joe had to yell at me a lot."

DiMaggio explained that it was only because of the crowd of 45,000 that he had had to do so much yelling. "The kid was all right," said Joe, which statement, coming from one of the game's greatest, was practically a rave notice.

On the subject of raves, Stengel leads the field for the kid. When Mantle rejoined the Yankees after his re-examination by his draft board, Casey wasted no time getting him into uniform for that afternoon's game against the Dodgers in Ebbets Field, even though Mickey had planed in from Kansas City that morning with a minimum of sleep.

"Boy never saw concrete before," tersely explained Stengel, who has a positive aversion to the use of proper names. By this pregame statement, the initiate understood that Ebbets Field would give Mantle his first experience in playing caroms off a concrete fence.

"I asked him if he wanted to play and he said, 'Yes,' so he's gonna play. Said to him, 'You cuddna got much sleep last night,' and he said, 'What difference does that make?' Guess mebbe at nineteen it doesn't.

"Told him not to worry about playing the ball off the wall out there. Told 'im I played the wall for six years and never had no trouble. He looked at me and said, 'Ya did?' Guess he thinks I was born at the age of sixty and started managin' immediately."

Writers who hadn't seen Mantle during spring training

besieged Stengel for an opinion as to the young man's worth. "Tell ya how it is," said Casey. "Some say he hits with more power right-handed, others say he hits with more power left-handed. Can't make up their minds. I hope they never find out which way he's the strongest.

"Course, he's a green pea in the outfield yet. He'll miss some fly balls. But on the other hand, he'll hit some nobody's gonna catch."

The Yankees opened the 1951 season with Mantle in right, DiMaggio in center and Jackie Jensen, the Rose Bowl footballer in left. It was an outfield, a press-box observer noted, "with 17 years of major-league experience, 16 of which belong to DiMaggio." Even that was an oversimplification for, while it was Joe's 1,621st major-league game, it was Jensen's 46th and Mantle's first.

Charley Berry, veteran American League umpire, who covered the long exhibition trail of the Yankees in 1951, gave it as his considered opinion that the performance of Mantle could be summed up in one word: "Amazing!"

"Unless you saw the things the boy did, you just wouldn't believe it," said Berry. "He hit balls, both in batting practice and in games, as far as I have ever seen a baseball hit. As much as I was impressed with his power and his speed, I was even more impressed with his poise. He certainly didn't act like a rookie up from Class C. He wasn't overanxious at the plate and frequently, when the pitcher had two strikes on him, Mantle would stay with him, lay off the bad pitches and wind up with a base on balls."

Mantle's first hint of the hazards of the spotlight came when the Yankees played an exhibition game against the University of Southern California on the USC campus. Di-

Maggio was excused early and, when the game ended, Mickey was mobbed for autographs by the students as he attempted to get into the bus carrying the Yanks from the ball field.

"Had DiMag been in the game until the end, he would have been the victim," related Ben Epstein of the New York *Daily Mirror*, "but with Joe gone, Mickey had no competition. The students, boys and girls, swarmed all over him. At one stage I thought the press of the crowd might tip over the bus. And the funny part of it was that Mickey was younger than most of the students."

One of Mantle's mightiest spring clouts was hit at Wrigley Field, Los Angeles, batting left-handed. The ball landed against a red-brick building in the right-center-field bleachers, a spot reached only eight or nine times in the history of the park, once by Babe Ruth in an exhibition game.

At Hollywood's Gilmore Stadium, Mickey took the fans by storm before the game ever started with his batting practice drives out of the park both right- and left-handed. Batting left-handed, Mantle hit eight into the boulevard behind the right-field fence, a territory safe from all but the lustiest of clouters.

At one of the Los Angeles games, Branch Rickey, Pittsburgh's big wheel, sat next to Dan Topping, Yankee president. Confessing himself fascinated by the levelness of Mantle's swing, the Mahatma passed a blank check to Dan and told him to fill in his own figures for the youngster. The gesture was undoubtedly theatrical, there being plenty of the old Belasco in Branch, but his praise of the rookie was sincere.

Mantle is one of five children. He has twin brothers, Ray and Roy, aged seventeen, who are athletes in their own right at

Commerce High; a sister, Barbara, fifteen, and a brother Larry, twelve.

As soon as the season was over and he was discharged from the hospital, Mantle returned to Commerce. When his knee mended sufficiently so that he was able to go on hunting trips, he decided it was time to do what he had been planning to do all year—get married. He took as a bride Miss Meryln Johnson, of nearby Picher, Oklahoma, whom he had known, by his own words, "since I was a kid in high school." That was all of four years ago.

Although still prone to striking out—he tied Larry Doby of Cleveland for the dubious distinction of leading the league in that department with 111—Mantle came into his own in 1952, a season saddened for him by the untimely passing of his dad.

Mickey took over Joe DiMaggio's vacated center field spot and played it better than anybody else on the Yankees could have and finished third in the league in hitting, with .311 and a total of 23 home runs. He belted two more in the World Series, batting .345 against the Dodgers.

By the time the 1953 season had rolled around, Mantle was being acclaimed as the new star of the American League. Brownie-manager Marty Marion called him a better ball player than Stan (The Man) Musial and Marty had been Stan's teammate for several years.

CHAPTER XIII

THE BIG CAT
(Johnny Mize)

BY TOM MEANY

When Lew Fonseca, director of promotion for the major leagues, unveiled his motion pictures of the 1951 World Series for their world premiere in New York early in January, 1952, he had an exceptional turnout. Every baseball figure within commuting distance of the city showed up, from Commissioner Ford C. Frick to the Ebbets Field ticket-sellers.

All the guests seemed unanimous in agreeing that Fonseca had done a remarkable job of catching the highlights of the six games between the Yankees and Giants, including Monte Irvin's steal of home and Eddie Stanky kicking the ball loose from Phil Rizzuto's glove in the third game.

Despite the general sense of a job well done, it was noticed that one man remained brooding for some time after the film had been finished. He was a Giant executive and certainly the stirring shots of the mobs pouring into the Polo Grounds should have stimulated him. He was asked what the trouble was.

"I just found out why we lost the Series," he muttered

morosely. "It was our pitchers—they pitched to Johnny Mize as if he were Babe Ruth, instead of Babe Ruth's cousin by marriage!"

A plea for further enlightenment brought forth the information that the Giant pitchers were too cautious toward Big Jawn, and that that had caused all the trouble.

"Mize!" repeated his listener incredulously, "Why Casey didn't use him until the last two games."

"Yeah," said the Giant official, "and they were the two games the Yankees won to win the Series. Look at it this way—what were the two most damaging hits made against the Giants?"

"Why, McDougald's grand-slam home run and Bauer's triple with the bases filled," replied the listener. "Anybody knows that."

"Sure," agreed the sore loser, "but you know what set them up, don't you? Bases on balls to Mize. In the fifth game at the Polo Grounds, the Yanks got men on second and third and two out. Mize gets an intentional pass from Larry Jansen and whammo!—McDougald hits into the seats. Two out again in the second game and the Yanks got men on second and third. This time Dave Koslo gets cute with Mize, pitches away from him and Johnny walks again. Then up comes Bauer and busts a triple up against the left field railing. Two bases on balls to Mize and it adds up to seven Yankee runs!"

The disgruntled Giant executive was historically correct but whether he was theoretically right is debatable. His specific charge was that the Giant pitchers had too much respect for Mize but somehow Big Jawn is a hitter who commands respect. Had Johnny been pitched to, he, too, might have unloaded the long ball. After all, with Joe DiMaggio retired,

Mize now has hit more home runs than any other active major leaguer—355.

It wasn't until Mize, after several formidable years with the Cardinals, came to New York that he gained his current nickname of "The Big Cat." In some ways, it is a misnomer for there is nothing in Johnny's play around first base which hints of feline grace. Facially, there may be a resemblance for Mize's red-tufted eyebrows and the cleft-chin at the base of his tapering face suggest a big Tom. And Mize certainly "guards" the plate with all the unblinking alertness of a cat watching a mouse-hole.

By his own admission, Johnny won't see forty again but he still has the same level swing which made him so feared in the National League for so many seasons. And still has American League pitchers chary of him. Mize isn't a .300 hitter any longer but he remains a home run threat. He hit 25 homers for the Yankees in 1950 and ten in 1951, including one as a pinch-hitter against no less a personage than Bob Feller of the Indians.

Not many major leaguers, however long their careers, hit over 300 home runs. DiMaggio and Mize played the same number of seasons and the Clipper, admittedly one of the greatest hitters of all time, has a bulge of ten on Big Jawn. Ted Williams, the Red Sox slugger, had 323 to his credit after the 1951 season.

Mize holds many interesting home run records. He is the only left handed hitter, except, of course, Babe Ruth, who has ever hit over 50 home runs. All the others who hit the half-century mark in homers were right handers, Ralph Kiner of Pittsburgh, Hank Greenberg of the Tigers, Jimmy Foxx, who did it with both the A's and Red Sox, and Hack Wilson of the Cubs.

Mize holds another mark—that of having hit three home runs in one game more often than any other player. Johnny turned this trick six times, including once with the Yankees when he was supposedly all washed up.

It was no novelty to Mize to find that the Giants considered him all through in August of 1949 when he came to the Yankees via the waiver route. He had been considered finished when the Cards sold him to the Giants a few days after Pearl Harbor. And as astute a judge of ball players as Larry MacPhail—and the red-head was a keen one, no matter what his critics say—considered Mize all through back in the mid-'30's.

When MacPhail was operating the Cincinnati Reds, he purchased Mize from the Cardinals on a conditional sale. In no time, he ordered Branch Rickey to take him back. A spur growth in Johnny's thigh convinced Larry that Mize's bones were so highly calcified that he was, in effect, turning to chalk.

As a matter of fact, the Yanks, desperate for pinch-hitting strength, picked up Mize in 1949 and thought he was finished the next season, when they sent him to Kansas City for therapy to his arm. Big Jawn had not been in the minors for 15 years but he lingered long enough in the American Association to hit .298, was recalled to the Yankees and biffed 25 home runs in 90 games.

Despite his great slugging, Mize never was in a World Series until he came to the Yankees. He had played with good clubs in St. Louis but either the Giants or Dodgers were always nosing them out for the pennant. In 1942, after he was traded away, the Cardinals won the flag. He played with a

Giant team in 1947 which set an all-time home run record of 221 and still wound up 13 games out of first place.

The rumor went around that Mize was not the type of ball player you could win a pennant with, although there was no evidence to support such a canard. The Cards had won in 1942 after getting rid of Johnny but they might have won *with* him in 1941 if he hadn't been injured and missed a couple of dozen games.

When Mize came to the Yanks in 1949, supposedly in the sere and yellow of his career, he got his first World Series chance. Stengel sent him up to bat against Preacher Roe of the Dodgers as a pinch-hitter in the second game, Brooklyn's only victory of the Series, and the Big Cat promptly singled to right.

The Series moved to Ebbets Field the next day and the game was 1-1 going into the top half of the ninth when the Yankees filled the bases with two out against Ralph Branca. Mize batted for Cliff Mapes and delivered what must have been the longest single in World Series history, a screaming drive that hit half way up on the screen atop the right field fence, drove in two runs. That hit drove out Branca and gave the Yanks a commanding lead.

Two solid singles in two pinch-hitting attempts were hardly what you'd expect of a fellow who was supposed to be a non-winning ball player.

Mize is an anomaly with the Yankees. Ordinarily, the club doesn't keep ball players who have passed 40, ball players who can't play a full season, ball players who aren't dependable fielders, ball players who can't run or throw. Big Jawn answers to all of these descriptions and the Yanks not only have him but they're paying him a good salary—about $25,000—and they have paid at least two other ball players, Joe Collins and Johnny Hopp, to share Johnny's labors around first base. Mize's value to the Yankees lies entirely in the fact that he is a menace to pitchers, a constant threat to deliver the long ball.

Despite being a heavy man, Mize is in as good physical shape as his years will permit. Golf and steam-baths constitute his conditional regimen and his only vice is that he is virtually a chain-smoker of cigars, no less. He admits it is a little tougher to go nine innings at first base than it used to be but Stengel nearly always has somebody on the bench to use in the closing innings.

Eventually Mize will be placed somewhere in the Yankee organization, probably as a minor league manager. The club respects him for the totally unexpected help he gave them when George Weiss gambled on him in late 1949, for the willingness with which he took a turn at Kansas City the next year and for his determination to give his employers all that he has left.

Coach Bill Dickey sees many years ahead for Mize. "With that swing of his, Johnny should be playing until he's almost 50," said Bill. "It's the easiest swing in baseball."

Quiet by nature, Mize has an amazing memory. He can recall details of games played many years ago—who batted after whom, which field the ball was hit to, what sort of pitch, what the count was, and so forth.

The placid Mize usually leaves everybody as unruffled as himself. The only time he ever stirs up any action among his teammates is when he quietly insists that Dizzy Dean was the greatest all around ball player he ever saw. Considering that

Big Jawn played with such men as Stan Musial, Mel Ott, Country Slaughter and Marty Marion in the National League and with Joe DiMaggio, Tommy Henrich and Phil Rizzuto in the American, it is a rare tribute he bestows on Dean. And Johnny was with Diz only a couple of seasons.

There is no doubht that Dean was one of the all-time pitching greats, but Mize insists he was a fine fielder and base-runner and by no means a bad hitter. Dizzy was, in fact, a co-ordinated ball player with skills in all departments. Mize's argument is not the less interesting because nobody can prove he is wrong, any more than he can prove he is right.

Mize broke in with Greensboro, North Carolina, in the Piedmont League in 1930 and made the usual rounds of the Cardinal chain-store system before winding up with the parent team in 1936. Eddie Dyer, who was the miracle manager of the Cardinals in 1946, says Johnny was exceptional from the very beginning.

"I used to be farm supervisor for Mr. Rickey," explained Dyer, "and it was our policy to congregate all of our lower minor league clubs in one spot for spring training. We had maybe 200 players at one such camp and I could have my back turned to the field and tell when Mize was hitting by the sound of the bat meeting the ball. Even when Johnny was a kid, his hits sounded different than anybody else's did. Sort of a ring of authority."

Mize's bat still has that ring of authority, even though Big Jawn himself can't get around as well as he used to. And he was no gazelle, even in his youth.

Mize married attractive Jene Adams in mid-season of 1937 and the young bride, on her honeymoon, will never forget the first time she saw Johnny play in New York. The Cardinals were playing at the Polo Grounds and Mize, on his second turn at bat, was conked squarely on the noggin and removed from the field on a stretcher.

From home plate to the center field clubhouse in the Polo Grounds is a long hike, almost 500 feet, and as the attendants made the long walk, the newly-wed Mrs. Mize made her dash from her seat behind the third base dugout. She had to circle the stands, go out into the street and approach the clubhouse from an outside entrance but she beat the stretcher-bearers there. It was with great relief that she learned all Johnny had sustained from the accident was a thumping headache.

Mize entered the Navy in 1943 after his first season with the Giants and missed three years which might have added to his home run string, but other home run sluggers such as DiMaggio and Williams were out of action in those seasons, too.

Mitz rose to great heights in the 1952 World Series. He hit three home runs, including one as a pinch-hitter, and was robbed of one which would have been the most dramatic of all by Carl Furillo's game-saving catch in the eleventh inning of the fifth game. Pressed into service after Brooklyn pitching had stopped Joe Collins cold, Big Jawn batted .400 and knocked in six runs, high for the Yankees. One of his most impressive hits was a single to left in the last game when Joe Black tried to fool him with a change of pace.

CHAPTER XIV

THE LITTLE CROW

(Jerry Coleman)

BY MILTON GROSS

The calloused precinct of a big-league clubhouse is hardly the place you would expect to find inspirational literature tacked on a dressing-room wall, or an established second-baseman pacing naked before his locker quoting *Strive and Succeed* phrases to himself.

You'll excuse the Yankees, however, if they no longer laugh or even smirk at Jerry Coleman, a composite Horatio Alger, All-American Boy, and Yankee Doodle Dandy with an overflowing measure of *Semper Fidelis*.

Coleman not only read such stuff in the clubhouse; he quoted it aloud, acted it out, swallowed it, and followed it. Some of his more crusty, hard-bitten teammates appeared to regard him and his quaint approach to the business of earning bread and butter out of baseball in a peculiar light. But they cannot discount the fact that milk-drinking Jerry chased snuff-eating George Stirnweiss off second base and to the St. Louis Browns while coming out of nowhere in 1949 to win The

Associated Press Rookie of the Year award, helping the Yankees to win the world championship, and then emerging in 1950 as an All-Star second-sacker and full-fledged World Series hero.

If, for example, Jerry's father, a former Pacific Coast League catcher who should know better, for his days in baseball date back to a recollection of rooming with Bob Meusel in the Arizona-Texas League, thinks Jerry needs the inspirational uplift of such pap—well, maybe he does. In 1950, during the frantic stretch run toward the flag, Coleman, Sr., kept sending Coleman, Jr., such letters from California.

Jerry would read them, with obvious emotion. Not too many words on them to take up too much of a man's time. Just enough to put the idea across. For instance there was one that just read, "Fight, Fight, Fight!" Another note exhorted Jerry to "Hang in there!" In a third, the father, who would have been regarded very peculiarly in his professional ballplaying days if he ever had uttered such exhortations aloud, charged the son to "Keep going. The way up is always rough."

After each such letter, Coleman strutted in front of his dressing cubicle reciting phrases to himself in the fashion of a Shakespearean actor rehearsing his lines. He would stop, take a batting stance, swing an imaginary bat, regard himself in the mirror, alter the stance a trifle, try the swing again, and then pick up the letter and mouth the inspirational clichés once more.

As a young man who had conclusively proven his ability to play championship baseball, Jerry was forgiven this strange personality twist by his teammates. Certainly, any rookie who can produce a double with the bases loaded in the final game of the season to beat the Red Sox out of the pennant and then collect five hits, including three doubles, in the Series—as Coleman did in 1949—is entitled to the luxury of being somewhat different. Especially when he proves it was no mistake by batting .287 and being an even bigger Series hero in his second season.

Coleman's leap from a mediocre minor-leaguer to one of the bright new stars of the majors was an astonishing feat. At Newark in 1948, Jerry hit .251. When he was brought to Spring training by the Yankees prior to the 1949 season, he had little doubt that they planned to place him in the showcase and peddle him along with other undesirable farm-hands. Of all the players in camp that Spring, Coleman was regarded as having the least chance to stick. His batting average was the lowest, he seemed too slim and retiring. There was so little to recommend him.

Coleman got his chance to demonstrate that he belonged only because Stirnweiss was hurt on the opening day of the season. In a fashion that beggared fiction, Jerry flubbed the first ball hit to him for an error, converted the next one into a double play, and thereafter did everything right. He had deliberately prepared himself for just such an opportunity. When it came, he was ready.

When the 1948 season had ended, Coleman concluded that he appeared to be headed nowhere in baseball. He resolved to give himself one more season and then, if he still faced a future as a confirmed minor-leaguer, he would quit and attempt to learn some business.

There was little else Jerry knew about at that point. There had been high school in San Francisco, baseball, and the war. Coleman did know, however, that even his approach to baseball had been all wrong. Never too strong, he found himself

15 pounds lighter at the end of each season than at the start, and so weary at the end of each game that he could barely go nine innings and had difficulty dragging himself to the clubhouse.

Yet, despite these obvious signs of physical weakness, Jerry had been the kind of hitter who grasped his bat at the very tip and swung for distance from the heels all the time. His glove and arm were keeping him in the high minors. His bat was preventing him from making the majors.

"During that Winter between 1948 and 1949, I thought it all out," Jerry says. "I had to strengthen my body and arms. I had to build up some sort of reserve of energy that I could call on when I needed that something extra on the field. I had to find some way to make my bat work for me instead of being a drag on me."

The way Jerry did it adds up to a page on which strong-man advertisements appear. "You, too, can look like this. Give me 15 minutes of your time each day and I'll prove it."

Jerry altered his way of life. He had been a heavy smoker. He gave up tobacco completely. He had never liked beer, but he knew that it would help to relax him and put some weight on his bones. He drank it. His appetite had been a constant concern. He decided that he had to force himself to eat more than he had been accustomed to. When he felt inclined to push himself away from the table, he stayed for at least a dozen more bites.

In the cellar of his home, Jerry rigged up a big mirror before which he could practice a new swing he had decided to employ. He bought a bat that was loaded with four pounds of lead and swung it 15 minutes each night. He purchased steel hand grips and set up a daily regime of flexing his fingers on the grips to strengthen the muscles of his hands. Each morning and evening, all through the Winter, he did 25 pushups.

Most important of all, however, was Jerry's decision to stop being extra-base crazy.

It's surprising that Jerry had delayed so long in concluding he wasn't destined to be a slugger. At Wellsville in the Pony League, in 1942, Jerry's first stop in organized baseball, he had seven bats broken in his first five games. At Kansas City, Binghamton, and Newark fast-ball pitchers invariably overpowered him. Some even knocked the wood out of his hands because he gripped the stick down at the knob of the handle.

"I guess it was watching Bobby Brown get his hits while choking up, even though he weighed 15 or 20 pounds more than I, that made up my mind for me," Jerry disclosed. "But that Winter, I moved my hands away from the handle and I've stayed that way ever since. I can't say that I'm sorry. I get a homer now and then, but I'm never swinging for the fences any more. The other way, I couldn't make it. This way, I have."

Even when he was considered among the Yankee indispensables, Coleman continued his body-building routine. Pushups were still a morning and evening ritual. Jerry also pep-talked himself at the plate and in the field. He carried on a running commentary designed to build up his own confidence and to chase away the blues when he boots one.

"I guess I'd sound silly if someone stepped up behind me and listened to what I say to myself," Jerry says, "but I find it helps me. When I'm batting, for example, I might say, 'Don't guess with him. If the pitch is over, hit it. Get out of the box now and look down for the sign.' Or maybe I'm in the field.

I might caution myself aloud. 'Careful of the hop. Watch your throw now. You almost threw that last one away. Give Phil a chance to get over to the base before you throw it.' "

Among his other novel approaches to cementing his place among the Yankee regulars, Jerry also devised variations of his batting stance for different kinds of pitchers. He refused to reveal his secret completely, but he does disclose that he changes the position of his feet in the batter's box and his crouch over the plate according to whether a pitcher is an overhand right-hander, a left-hander, or a hurler who throws a slider.

Jerry rarely has anything on his mind except baseball. He admits he has no other interest. If he plays golf, it's for the fresh air, not the score, which rarely runs below 100 when Jerry is shooting. If he reads a book, he skims and gazes rather than absorbs what is passing before his eyes. He is not a fisherman or a hunter, the outdoor sports which dominate the off-season for so many players.

"I guess I've just never had the time to become interested in anything other than baseball," Jerry explains.

Jerry is a native of San Francisco, California. He was born in San Jose on September 14, 1924, but only because his mother's doctor lived there, he explains. As soon as his mother was discharged from the hospital, she took him back to the town he has called home ever since.

It was there, in the recreation parks, that Coleman was to form the friendships and the love for baseball that was to govern every minute of his life, not excluding the years while he was piloting a Marine dive-bomber and dreaming of getting out of the service to try for a career in baseball.

Jerry was about 14 years old when he met up with Bobby Brown, Bill Wight, Carl DeRose, Dino Restelli, and Charley Silvera, other baseball-crazy kids who were to oppose each other in high school but play together on a semi-pro team known as the Keneally Yankees. As a sophomore of 15, weighing 145 pounds, Jerry made the Lowell High School varsity.

With the Keneally team, and in Lowell High school, Jerry had three boosters—plus himself, naturally. As Brown, Coleman's Yankee teammate, tells the story, "There were only four people who ever thought Jerry would become a big-leaguer. They were Jerry himself, his father, me, and the late Joe Devine."

"That's just about the size of it," Coleman agrees, "and of the four of us, I guess Devine carried more weight and was more important than I was myself in getting me where I am today."

Devine was the Yankee scout, a fatherly man with a pleasant manner who was responsible for the dozen Californians on the Yankees. It was Devine who first touted Tony Lazzeri. It was Devine who stamped the okay on Joe DiMaggio, although others were afraid that DiMag's knee was chronically bad.

Devine saw something in Jerry that nobody else did. Coleman could not hit too well, even for the sandlots, but there was a touch of the big time in his fielding even as a 15-year-old and there was an easy grace in his manner and a studied care in the way he carried himself that made it look as though nothing could touch the kid once he put on his spikes and glove.

"You'll make the big league for me," Devine told Jerry, and made a verbal agreement with the youngster to sign with the Yankees' Wellsville farm even before Coleman had graduated from high school.

In mid-June of 1942, Jerry was sent down to the Pony League after his graduation. It was there that he envisioned himself a long-ball hitter and almost brought about the eventual ruin of his career at its very inception. Coleman compiled a .304 average for half a season before enlisting in the Navy V-5 aviation program and volunteering for Marine Corps duty.

Not once in the next three years did Coleman have the privilege of touching a bat, a glove, or a baseball. Instead, he handled the controls of an SBD (Dauntless) or an SB 2C (Helldiver) as a bomber pilot. Jerry flew 57 strikes in the Solomons and Philippines, coming out of the service as a 1st Lieutenant with a chest full of decorations.

It came as something of shock to the Yankee brass, therefore, when the Marine Corps in January, 1952, recalled Jerry, who held a reserve commission. It had been assumed that because of his service in World War II Coleman would not be called up again.

Jerry put in six months at the University of San Francisco, but his mind wasn't on school work any more than it was on anything else except making the grade with the Yankees. Devine was still there, talking up his boy to farm head George Weiss.

Jerry was sent into Spring training with Kansas City in 1946, but was optioned to Binghamton and played about 30 games at third base, 80 at shortstop, and 20 at second base, under Lefty Gomez. On the strength of his .275 average, Coleman was promoted to Kansas City. There, under Billy Meyer, Jerry was figured as a third-baseman. He played 100 games at the far corner and was used at shortstop only after Odie Strain was injured.

Coleman had his first look at a Yankee camp at St. Petersburg in 1948, after hitting .278 at Kansas City. But there was no place for Jerry with the varsity yet. He was sent down to Newark, where he had his worst year in the Yankee chain, concentrating once again at shortstop. Once more, Jerry was used around the infield, however, so that by the end of the season he had added perhaps 30 more games at second base to give him a total-game second-base experience of, perhaps, 50 games in the minor leagues.

The off-season was a depressing time for Jerry. He had married a childhood sweetheart two years before and he felt that time was slipping by without the promise of a fruitful future. Jerry might have decided to quit baseball right then but Devine, as usual, was handy to talk him out of it. Give it another year or so, Joe urged Jerry.

Meanwhile, Devine had Casey Stengel's ear, and perhaps, here is the biggest break Coleman could possibly have obtained. On the West Coast, Devine, through the years, had been in contact with the home office only through long-distance telephone, occasional letter, and a semi-annual visit with George Weiss. Either Devine would go East or George go West.

But here, finally, was Stengel appointed Yankee manager for the 1949 season, living in Glendale, California, near enough for Devine to have Casey's ear all Winter. What Devine preached so far as Jerry was concerned, added up to this: "Disregard the record. Disregard everything you've heard about this kid. I know he can make it. Try him. Just take him South and look at him where he can do the team the most good.

Shortstop? No, Rizzuto's there. Third base? What's with Brown and Billy Johnson? Second base? Hasn't played there much, but the kid's an acrobatic kind of player. He's frisky as a colt in the field, reminds you a lot of Crosetti. He's got his mannerisms. Goes down into the dirt for a ball the same way, runs just like him too, although I don't think he ever saw The Crow play. Case, try this kid. He'll help you."

When Devine referred to Crosetti as "The Crow," he wasn't belittling the Yankee coach, for Frankie had been one of the late Yankee scout's most prized discoveries. The ball players always called Frank "Crow" as a shortening of his full name of Crosetti.

And Devine was 100 per cent correct when he said Coleman had all of Crosetti's mannerisms, even though he had never seen him play. The resemblance in the field is so marked that the Yanks promptly dubbed Jerry "The Little Crow."

Thus it was that, unknown to veteran correspondents covering the Yankee Spring camp in 1949, Stengel had his eye on Coleman as a prospective second-sacker. And then Stirnweiss, who had been a drag on the varsity in 1948, underwent a rebirth. He was the team's outstanding Spring hitter. His weight was down. He hustled. He looked like the Snuffy of 1944 and 1945. On the second day of the season, he was hurt.

It was a bad break for Stirny, but the chance of a lifetime for Coleman. There were so many things he did not know about second base, but he learned them in the heat of competition by asking questions.

There probably isn't a player in the leagues today with so curious a mind and tongue as Coleman. He harassed Stirnweiss with questions his first few weeks of the 1949 season and it's to Snuffy's credit that he helped Jerry all he could. Once Coleman grabbed coach Jim Turner, as he was to do so many more times as the season progressed.

"How would you pitch to me?" Coleman wanted to know.

It was the kind of question Turner was glad to hear from the rookie, who looked so much like a young college graduate, for it indicated to Jim that Coleman had the inquisitive mind that must reap dividends in baseball. Where once Brown and Crosetti had made a strange duo moving about together when the Yankees were on the road, Coleman now joined this seminar in infield play, with Crosetti instructing both youngsters at the dinner table, during a walk to a movie, or sitting about a hotel room.

How well he learned his lessons is seen in his handsome .287 batting average for 1950, an improvement of 12 points over his freshman mark, and in his brilliant performance in the World Series against the Phillies. Coleman was a thorn in the side of the Philadelphia club all through the four-game sweep by the Yankees, and climaxed his efforts by driving in the winning run in the crucial third game, won by the New Yorkers, 3-2.

Jerry went on the Riggs-Jachym barnstorming tour after the 1950 Series. It ended prematurely in Miami and he headed home for California—and a Winter of vigorous exercise. Unlike many ballplayers, Coleman refuses to spend the off season in complete relaxation. He starts preparing for Spring training as soon as he gets back in San Francisco.

Extremely friendly, and the type who laughs and smiles easily, black-haired Coleman also is on the bashful side. He embarrasses easily, but is of such a fortunate nature that he is able to take a joke against himself and turn it to good advantage. Jerry's 26-year-old brunette wife claims she knows nobody who has so refreshing a sense of humor where he himself is the butt of a story. To illustrate her point, Louise urged Jerry to tell about his experience on the golf links in 1950 when he played in a baseball players' tourney for a California charity.

"I guess it was funny, after all," Coleman said as his lips creased in the characteristic grin that lights up his handsome face so often. "I finished so far behind everybody else, it really seemed like a gag. It took me three swings to get off the tee, and when I finally got some distance to the ball, it almost knocked a fellow out of a hamburger stand a little bit off the course. It was all for charity, so what did I care."

"You know," said Mrs. Coleman, "it *is* possible to live with him. He isn't much more than twice the trouble of Diane Louise. That's our baby daughter."

It's just that Jerry is a prissy sort of person, strange for a ballplayer. He does not like steak, for instance. He prefers casserole dishes, which automatically classes him among baseball's unorthodox. Jerry also is the kind of husband who gladly goes shopping with his wife. He buys most of his own clothes—and on him they look good.

At home, Louise complains, Jerry is no help whatsoever. He always manages to find something of his own to do when there are house chores waiting. But when birthdays and anniversaries come around, Jerry remembers them, not just by a verbal greeting but with gifts that delight a wife's heart.

Coleman likes to sing, but can't carry a tune, his wife says. She boasts about his marvelous rhythm when he dances with her, but decries the fact that during the baseball season he becomes so tired they rarely are able to go dancing.

"But," Jerry reminds her, "I'm a ball player, not a ballroom dancer. I can't think of any way I'd rather get tired than playing baseball. I'm thankful I was able to get the chance."

That's just about what Jerry also told Manager Stengel while the Yankees were celebrating their 1949 World Series triumph over the Dodgers.

Champagne flowed freely. There was hardly a dry eye in the place when Coleman cornered Stengel at one point in the evening and said soberly, "Thanks for giving me the chance to play, Skipper. I hope I never disappoint you."

"You're thanking me?" Casey echoed, his wizened face wreathed with his victory smile. "I gotta thank you. I gotta thank Devine for talking to me about you. I gotta thank myself for listening to him. Disappoint me, kid? You made me the manager of the world champions. Nobody ever did that kind of a favor for me before."

CHAPTER XV

"THEY ALSO SERVE"
(The Coaches)

BY ARCH MURRAY

Under a lot of managers coaches are obscure and unimportant citizens, hard-working old ball-players who slip further and further into the back-ground with each passing year. Only rarely do you hear of them and usually when you do it is because they have pulled a rock of some kind that has cost their team a big ball-game. Hardly anybody in Brooklyn, for example, knew who Milt Stock was until that fatal autumn afternoon in 1950 when he made his classic blunder of waving home Cal Abrams, who carried the potential winning run in the ninth inning of the final game of the year with a pennant in the balance, when he didn't have a chance to make it.

Stock's chief claim to fame prior to that had been the fact that he was Eddie Stanky's father-in-law. But thereafter in Brooklyn he became known as the "guy who cost us the pennant in 1950" and Stock's rock took its place among the tragic blunders of baseball history. Milt, a thoroughly sound and shrewd coach, blew his job for that one mistake and he would gladly exchange that moment in the headlines for the obscurity that is the normal lot of big league coaches. There have been other luckier coaches who toiled for years hardly ever seeing their names in public print. The manager takes all the bows and all the blame. Art Fletcher, Joe McCarthy's top aide, liked it that way. He turned down a chance to manage the Yankees after Miller Huggins' death in 1929 because he'd had a whirl at managing and he didn't like it. "It just isn't worth the headaches," was his succinct comment.

Under McCarthy the Yankee coaches were silent, unsung characters. Fletcher and Earle Combs did their jobs well and faithfully. They were vital cogs in those mighty Yankee machines who won eight pennants under old Marse Joe. But they stayed in the shadows and let McCarthy absorb all the praise and the raps, too. The story's different today, though. Casey Stengel leans heavily on his coaches—Bill Dickey, Jim Turner, Frankie Crosetti and Tommy Henrich—and admits it frankly. Henrich, of course, severed his connections with the club after 1951 but the other three remain vibrant parts of the Yankee scheme and Ol' Case insists they receive the plaudits share and share alike with the old professor himself.

"The Yankees," Casey has said over and over again, "are no one-man brain trust. Sure, I make the final decisions but actually we work as a team. I won't have any yes-man coaching for me. We all pool our ideas and I'm the first guy to accept their suggestions. You writer guys have called me a lot of things in the past four years, ranging all the way from lucky stiff to miracle manager. But I'll tell you one thing. I doubt if we could have won four pennants in a row without my coaches. I say they're the best in the world and the records certainly don't dispute me. Bill and Jim and Frankie and for one year Tommy all did their part. I just can't give them enough credit. All I know is Ol' Case wouldn't be taking the bows if it hadn't been for them."

To understand the importance of the current Yankee coaches you must first remember that they are all old Yankees —two of them, Dickey and Crosetti, superstars during the greatest era of Yankee greatness and the other, Turner, a crafty old relief pitcher during the war years. They have all heard the roar of the Stadium crowds and they all know what it means to be a Yankee. That is an important point to remember for Casey's battle-cry ever since he came to the Stadium in 1949 to replace Bucky Harris has been one which stresses the greatness of the Yankee tradition.

He keeps infusing the younger Yankees of today with the thought that it is great to be a Yankee. "Don't ever forget," he has told his players repeatedly, "once you put on that shirt with the Yankee emblem on it, you become a Yankee and you stay a Yankee. Great things are expected of you just because you are wearing that uniform. Don't ever let it down. If you do you won't be a Yankee long."

Casey, of course, wasn't the first to sing that it's great to be a Yankee. That was Waite Hoyt, a great right-hander under Miller Huggins in the twenties. Hoyt was the first to say that "it's great to be young and a Yankee." Then in 1930 after Hug died and the mighty Yankee powerhouse that reigned through '26, '27 and '28 had begun to come apart at the seams he added a postscript. "The trouble," he said of the struggling 1930 array managed by Bob Shawkey, "with this Yankee team is they're not enough Yankees." He was right, too, and ironically he wasn't to remain one long himself for shortly after he uttered those memorable words he was shipped to Detroit.

But if Hoyt started it, Casey has carried the torch of tradition high ever since he moved into the Bomber pilot room. The first thing he did was to name three old Yankee stars as his coaches. One of them, of course, had never left them. That was Crosetti, the lithe and agile shortstop who arrived the year after McCarthy. Crosetti was the second of the fabulous Italian triumvirate who came out of San Francisco to help write many a golden page into the Yankee ledgers. Tony Lazzeri, of course, was the first and the third was the marvelous Joe DiMaggio, who rounded out 13 brilliant Yankee years in the fall of 1951.

Crosetti was least colorful of this mighty trio. He was a strange paradox of a player and even in the maturity of his coaching years he remains a paradox. On the field he is a lively chatter-box who can tangle with the best of the bench jockeys around the league. Off the field he is the quietest of all ballplayers. The Pirates used to claim that Arky Vaughan, their great shortstop, said hello in the spring and never spoke again until he said good-bye in the fall. But Crosetti goes him one better. He just shakes hands and nods.

Somebody said once that Crosetti was an ideal Yankee. His whole life is baseball. He lives, eats and breathes it. Save for his family, he has no other interests. He has always been the first Yankee to bed and the first in the dining room in the morning. His vocal output off the field remains constantly at an irreducible minimum. The only evidence that betrays the emotional fires stoked inside him is a rare flare of temper on the field or a shy and bashful smile that lights up his whole face. Otherwise, he is a somber, poker-faced little guy who goes quietly about his business in thorough and painstaking fashion.

It's no mere coincidence that young infielders coming up to the Yankees develop so fast. Twice in the past four years the Yankees have produced the rookie of the year and the fact that both were infielders is a tribute to the coaching guile of the slick and silent man from the hills of colorful San Francisco. In 1949, a kid named Jerry Coleman joined the Yankees at St. Petersburg with the old tag of good-field-no-hit upon him. It was acknowledged that he was a great glove but in three full seasons in the top minors he'd never hit better than .278. The year before at Newark he'd hit only .251. He didn't appear to be a Yankee with a bat in his hands. The Yankees didn't seem to have too much need for him, either, as they had a good second baseman in George Stirnweiss. Snuffy had been a batting champion during the war and he'd remained good enough to chase Joe Gordon off to Cleveland in the trade for Allie Reynolds at the end of the 1946 season.

That was the kind of a ball player Coleman was being asked to beat out. It seemed like an utter impossibility. But Crosetti liked the way Jerry glided around the infield dirt with a glove of magic and he took him in hand. He gave him a few batting tips and taught him a few tricks of the infield trade. Stirnweiss broke a finger in the first week of the season and by the time he was ready to play again he'd lost his job to the young and sensational Coleman. Snuffy never got it back, either. Coleman hit .275 that freshman season, fielded brilliantly and played a vital role in the whomping of the Dodgers in the World Series. It came as no surprise at all when he was named the rookie of the year.

Two years later another unsung kid turned up at the Yankee camp. True, he'd been a sensational hitter under Rogers Hornsby at Beaumont in the Texas League in 1950 but he'd never played anywhere but second base and nobody was going to beat out Coleman. That was the thought when the Yankees arrived in Phoenix in February but Casey Stengel took one look at him and liked what he saw.

"I don't know," Casey said in his first press conference under the Arizona sun, "but this kid Gil McDougald looks good to me. I'm going to try him at third base. It looks as though we aren't going to have Bobby Brown. He's interning in a hospital in San Francisco and the Army is almost sure to grab him. That leaves me with only Bill Johnson at third and Billy isn't getting any younger. Maybe the kid can do the job for me."

Casey looked up and winked. "And I'll tell you another thing," he added. "If the kid can't make it at third and he's as good a second baseman as they say he is, I wouldn't be afraid to move Coleman to third. I know he can play there."

But with Crosetti teaching him, Gil caught on at third in a hurry—so well that the Yankees sold Bill Johnson to the Cards in May. He led the club in hitting as a rookie with a .306 average and by season's end he had made a part-time player out of the great Coleman. When Brown finally decided to play a little ball before the Army took him, Casey decided to make the most of his hitting and McDougald's versatility. So Gil played third against left-handers and second against right-handers with either Coleman or Brown sitting on the bench. Once again the crafty Crosetti had applied the polish that for the second time in two years had made a raw Yankee infielder the rookie of the year.

Crosetti operates on the third base coaching lines—a vastly under-rated job. The word around the Yankee clubhouse is that Frankie has yet to make a mistake in judgment at that testing post. The men in the trade say that the third base coaching job is one of the toughest in the business. "Only a guy with a really sharp mind can do the job, "insists Al Schacht, the restaurateur who was a pretty fair third base coach himself before he quit the lines to corral vast gobs of greenbacks as the Clown Prince of Baseball. "He can't afford to make a mistake, especially in a tight game, and he has to think of a million things at the same time. He has to figure the speed of the runner, the break he got from second, how hard the ball was hit and just where, the position of the outfielder and the strength of his arm. He has to know the condition of the turf so as to judge how the ball will bounce. And he has to think of all these things at once with the runner going at top speed. He can't hesitate for the slightest let-up might mean the guy would be out at the plate. The job calls for lightning reflexes and split-second timing as well as the guts of a paratrooper. And if you really want to know, there aren't too many really good ones around."

But Frankie is one of them. He's one of the most valuable of all the Yankees despite the fact that his playing days are well behind him. He was a great shortstop in his day, too. Joe McCarthy was quick to recognize that. "You know," he said once as a Yankee train was rolling west toward St. Louis and a World Series, "the most under-rated guy on this team is Frankie Crosetti. They rave about DiMag and Dickey and Keller and Henrich. They talk about the great pitching. But you never hear a word about Frank and he's one of the big reasons we keep on winning. I've always said that no team is any better than its shortstop. You check back through the records and you'll find that no team ever won a pennant without a good one. And don't forget what I'm telling you. Frankie is one of the very best."

The record books say that Crosetti wasn't a great hitter. His lifetime batting average for 17 Yankee years was only .249 and he never went over .290 in the big leagues. But that hardly tells the story. He was a deadly clutch hitter and he was always at his best with the big runs on the bases in an important game. He hit only 98 home runs during his active span as a Yankee but most of them came at vital times. He played in seven World Series and 29 Series games and hit only one homer in the lot. But they'll never forget that one. It came off Dizzy Dean in the eighth inning at Chicago in 1938 and ruined one of ol' Diz's greatest and gamest efforts. Diz was way over the hill then and his fast ball was a thing for the memory books but he had the Yankees swinging in utter futility until Frankie broke his heart and the Cubs' backs with one swipe of his big brown bat.

Frankie was the lead-off man for those powerhouse Yankee teams of Joe McCarthy and he possessed the invaluable Stanky-type knack of getting on base ahead of the big belters. With Red Rolfe, one of the great number two hitters in history, batting right behind him, followed by such clouters as DiMaggio, Gehrig, Keller and Dickey it was no wonder that the Bombers kept those runs pouring over the plate. Frankie had a sharp eye and he drew a lot of walks. But his most singular gift was his uncanny ability to get hit by a pitched ball without damaging anything save the rival pitcher's composure. He still holds the major league record of leading the league in the little matter of hit by pitcher for five straight years. In all, it was no wonder that Joe McCarthy called him the most under-rated Yankee of them all.

Across the diamond from Frankie when the Yanks take their bats in hand is a tall, lean man with graying temples. He has been a dominant figure in the Stadium scene for the better part of a quarter of a century. Big Bill Dickey, the Arkansas Alp as he was known in his playing days, was one of the three greatest catchers of the modern era. Mickey Cochrane of the A's and Tigers and Gabby Hartnett of the Cubs were the other two. Young old-timers will still argue far into the night as to who was the best. It's pretty tough to split them out for they were all great in their own dynamic ways. But certainly Dickey was the greatest catcher ever to wear a Yankee uniform and there are those who insist he was the man who made the Bombers tick. "He's the key man," Clark Griffith, the Old Fox of the Senators who spent many a sleepless night trying to find a chink in the Yankee armor, used to say. "He's the one who makes the difference." Griffith could have been right, too, for the year Dickey went away to join the Navy was the year the Yankees stopped winning. They had won seven pennants in eight years from 1936 through 1943. But after Dickey departed they weren't to win again until 1947 when a new team of Yankees had been built.

Dickey joined the Yankees in the fall of 1928 when the dynasty wrought by little Miller Huggins was reaching the end of its run. In his first appearance at the plate as a Yankee old Red Faber of the White Sox struck him out. But that didn't bother either Hug or Dickey. Hug, tired and worn with a great team aging before his eyes, sensed that Dickey and Lou Gehrig would be the foundation on which a new and greater Yankee powerhouse would be built. Dickey became the first-string catcher the next spring at St. Pete and one of the top legacies the little leader left behind when he died the following fall. For the next 13 seasons, Bill caught 100 or more games—a record still unmatched. For his 16 active Yankee years he had a lifetime batting average of .313. He reached his peak in 1937 when he caught 140 games, batted .332, hit 29 home runs and 35 doubles and knocked in 133 runs. But he still thinks his greatest thrill came in 1943—his last full season as a Yankee player. He was 36 years old then and heading into the sunset. The war had started to take the toll of the Yankees that year. Joe DiMaggio, Tommy Henrich, Phil Rizzuto and Buddy Hassett had all gone into the service and Red Rolfe, the great third baseman, had been forced to call it quits due to the ravages of a severe case of colitis. But the Yankees still had Keller and Joe Gordon, Spud Chandler and Tiny Bonham—and Dickey. They had the rookie of the year at third base in Bill Johnson. Nick Etten, a first baseman bought from the Phillies, finished second to Rudy York in runs batted in. The Bombers beat Washington in the season's opener and were never headed. They won the flag by 11 games over the Senators and got their chance to gain revenge on the Cards in the World Series. (Billy Southworth's fleet youngsters had beaten them in five games the year before.)

They won two of the first three games at the Stadium and then swung west to St. Louis. Marius Russo outlasted Max Lanier in a tight pitching duel in the fourth game at Sportsmans Park, 2-1, to give the Yanks a 3-1 grip on the Series. But they still had one more to win and Mort Cooper, the guy who had beaten them in the second game the day his father had died, was a tough man to get by. It was a tight scoreless duel going into the sixth with Chandler holding off the Redbirds and the Yankees unable to break through Cooper. But then Keller lashed a bouncing single to right and Dickey, coming through as he had so often in the past, blasted a home run onto the pavilion roof in right field for the only runs of the game. "That was the greatest of them," says Bill, looking back. "It was my last big blow for the Yankees and the sweetest, too."

Bill spent the next two years in the Navy and when he got out the whispers swirled that he was through with baseball. He would be 39 that June of 1946 and it looked like too tough a job. But Bill told Larry MacPhail, who had taken over the Yankees from Ed Barrow and the Ruppert estate the year before, that he wanted to give it a try. He was a far cry from the old Dickey but he caught 31 of the club's first 38 games. Late in May Joe McCarthy, his old gall bladder trouble kicking up again and his nerves a wreck, resigned after 16 years at the Yankee helm. He left behind him a record of eight pennants and seven world championships. Dickey was named to replace him.

The Yankees, stumbling and faltering, were five games back of the Red Sox when Bill took over. And in the 100 days of his managerial tenure they fell further and further behind. DiMaggio, only a shadow of his pre-war self, hit under .300 for the first time in his career. Tommy Henrich hit only .251 and Joe Gordon far below that. The club as a whole hit only .240 during Dickey's days at the helm and there was nothing Bill could do. Writers traveling with the club that year thought he did a great job to keep the club as high as third under the circumstances but apparently MacPhail didn't agree. He refused to give Dickey a vote of confidence and in Detroit on the last western trip Bill told the press that he didn't wish to be considered for the managerial job in 1947. That irked MacPhail and he fired Dickey the next day, appointing Johnny Neun to finish out the season.

Everybody, Dickey included, thought that was the end of Dickey as a Yankee. And it might have been but for that famous day in June in 1948 when the Yankees celebrated the silver anniversary of the Stadium and Babe Ruth, only two months away from the end of the road, made his final appearance at the great arena he helped so much to build. Called back with the rest of the old Yankee greats, Bill donned his old uniform again and felt a nostalgic yearning for the days that were gone. Afterwards he told George Weiss that he'd like to come back to the Yankees in some capacity if there ever was an opening. Weiss didn't forget and the next winter when Casey Stengel was picking his coaches the Yankee boss told him that Dickey might be available. Case leaped to the phone and in a few brief minutes Bill was back with the Bombers as a coach.

In the light of what's happened since then, that was one of the smartest moves Stengel ever made. For it was Dickey who made Yogi Berra into the catcher he had promised to be.

Bill took Yogi under his wing that spring of 1949 at St. Petersburg and the transformation was all but incredible. Ever since the 1947 World Series when the Dodgers had run wild on him and forced him to the bench in the final game, Yogi had been tagged as a catcher who couldn't throw. But Dickey didn't agree. "He has a marvelous arm," Dickey said that March under the Florida sun. "His great fault is that he tries to throw too soon without getting a proper grip on the ball. I'm teaching him to get set before he throws. Let the runner get a stride extra. A good throw will get him, anyway. Yogi says his fingers are too short. But I tell him he should have seen Mickey Cochrane's."

Yogi, agreeing that Dickey was "learning me his experience," came fast under Bill's tutelage. His strong, sure throws nailed enemy runners in their tracks and his handling of pitchers became sharper and surer. His hitting took up the slack of the fading outfield trio of Charley Keller, Tommy Henrich and DiMag. He hit the long ball and he belted home the runs. He got better every year and in 1951 he was voted the most valuable player in the league. The wonders Dickey wrought with the squat man from "The Hill" in St. Louis were tribute enough to his coaching talents.

But in 1951 Dickey came up with another great bit of help. The first base situation would have been grim indeed if Dickey hadn't revised Joe Collins' hitting style and made him into a dangerous swatter who broke up many a game for the Yankees despite his low average. "In the fall of 1950," Collins recalls, "Bill told me that I'd have to change things around if I was to stick with the Yankees. He told me I was holding the bat too far forward to swing the bat properly. He made me spread my feet and moved me around at the plate so that instead of facing third I almost had one foot in the bucket in the direction of first. This way I get a better look at the ball and because my bat's way back on my shoulders I don't have to commit myself and offer at a ball until I'm sure it's the one I want to hit. It's enabled me to get the full use of my power."

Dickey had helped the other Yankee hitters, too, including Gene Woodling. He taught Woodling how to pull and it was Gene's home runs against Cleveland that broke the back of the Indian pennant threat. Bill helped the aging DiMag out of one slump after another, thereby keeping him in the lineup so that the pitchers could get the full use of his still wondrous fielding. All in all, the great Yankee catcher is still pulling a mighty oar for the Yankees he served so well as the iron man in a mask.

Third and far from least of the surviving Yankee coaching trio is James Riley Turner, the old milkman from Antioch, Tennessee. Jim is in complete charge of the Yankee pitchers and Casey would be the first to tell you that pitching is what has carried the Bombers over the hump of four straight bitter pennant fights. Time and again, writers wandering into the Yankee dugout before a game will ask Casey who's going to pitch the next day and they'll get the same answer. "I don't know," Case'll say, "I haven't talked to Jim." Or maybe it will be just a laconic "Ask Turner."

There's nothing fussy or fancy about old Jim. He learned about pitching the hard way. He knocked around in the bushes for 14 years before he got his first chance in the big leagues at the age of 32. He might never have gotten that chance but for the fact that Donie Bush offered him to Bob Quinn, then the boss of the poverty-stricken Braves, for a song in 1937. "The guy's been knocking around for a long time," Bush told his old friend, "and he knows all there is about pitching. I'd like to see him get a chance up there. But nobody will give him one because of his age. Tell you what I'll do. You give him a shot and I'll let you have him for $500."

Quinn, desperate for ball-players and knowing that almost anybody was worth a gamble at that price, agreed. Old Jim didn't let him down. In his freshman year in the big

leagues he won 20 games for the second-division Braves and
tacked up an earned run average of 2.38. He spun six shut-outs
that year and in one span put together 31 straight scoreless
innings. He never was quite that good again but he was good
enough. Traded to the Reds at the end of the '39 season he
won 14 games for Bill McKechnie, his manager at Boston in
his rookie season, and played a large role in the winning of
the pennant in 1940. The years were catching up with him
now, though, and in midseason of 1942 he was shipped to
Newark. That was his first affiliation with the Yankees and
it proved to be a lucky one for all parties involved. Brought
up to the Stadium when the manpower shortage began to take
its toll, he served as a shrewd and crafty relief pitcher through
the rest of the war years. He was crowding 40 then but through
those lean years he played an important role in keeping the
Yankee record of not having finished in the second division
since 1925 intact. Old Jim saved a lot of games for the faltering
Yankee starters and he might have saved others but for the
shoddy defenses behind him.

When the war ended and the stars of the game came home,
the Yankees showed the 42-year-old Turner their appreciation
for his efforts when the going was rough. They made him
manager at Beaumont, their Texas League farm. He did a
good job there in '46 and they moved him up a notch to Portland in the Pacific Coast League the next year. It was at Portland in 1947 that Turner applied the final touches to the
pitcher who has been Mr. Pork Chops for the Yankees during
their last three pennant-winning years. Raschi was 28 when
the Yankees shipped him to the Coast League that spring and
at first he was loath to go. He wasn't getting any younger and

his future seemed clouded with doubt. But George Weiss persuaded him that Turner would make him into a big leaguer and he finally agreed to head west.

In two months, Jim had sharpened his curve and had turned him from a completely overhand pitcher into one who could throw with a three-quarter and even underhand delivery. That was what made the difference. And it showed right away. He won eight and lost but two for the Beavers before he was recalled to shore up Bucky Harris' sagging mound staff in July. He won seven games for the Bombers down the stretch, making a big difference in the drive for the pennant. He won 19 games for Harris in 1948 but that wasn't quite enough with the other pitchers staggering and the Yankees bowed out of the flag race on the next to the last day of the season. In four pennant-winning years since he has won 79 and lost 34. Over a six-year span he is the top percentage pitcher in baseball with 105 victories and 36 defeats and a .745 percentage. No post-war pitcher in baseball has had a better mark. His reward has been that in 1952 with Joe DiMaggio gone he became the highest paid Yankee—higher than Phil Rizzuto, Yogi Berra or any of the other touted Yankee stars.

Raschi is Turner's greatest contribution to the Yankee cause but Jim has been a great help to all the Yankee pitchers. Allie Reynolds insists that he never capitalized on his full potential until Turner arrived at the Stadium in 1949. "Jim taught me plenty," says the Chief who was voted the player of the year by the New York chapter of Baseball Writers for the 1951 season. "I had the idea that all you had to do to win when you had a good strong arm was to blow the batter down. But Jim taught me the little lesson of not giving in to the batter too quick. Before Jim came along I wouldn't try to fool the batter but would come in with the ball he wanted and challenge him to hit it. Now I try to keep nibbling away at the hitters until they're the ones who have to swing at what I give them or be counted out. It's as simple as this. Earlier I was giving the hitters their pitch to hit; now I make them hit mine."

Big Jim was Stengel's first coaching choice when he was named manager. Casey had seen Turner handle pitchers at Portland when they were both in the Coast League in 1948 and he knew that Jim was his type of guy. "He and I," Casey said when Turner got the job, "see eye to eye in the matter of hurling technique and the handling of pitchers." That has been well borne out. For no pitching coach in memory ever was so completely in charge of things as Turner has been since he came back to the Stadium.

Turner is an old-fashioned pitcher with solid, basic ideas. He is a philosopher and a student first of the men who make up his staff and then of the art of pitching itself. "I'm no glamor boy," Jim insists. "I have no great bag of tricks. But there isn't a pitcher in the big leagues with an ounce of brains in his skull who wouldn't delight in the chance I've had with the Yankees. I've been given free leeway to work out my own ideas—my own quirks and notions—with the Yankee staff. That's any pitcher's dream.

"There's no great secret about pitching. The one basic thing is control and that's what I'm always aiming for in my pitchers. Here's what I mean by control. You hear people say that a certain guy can't get it over. They are speaking in terms of the relationship of the pitched ball and the plate. But they're wrong. Because anybody can throw a baseball over the plate. The big trick is to be around the plate, to get that hair-line control so you can master the corners and throw that low strike. And don't forget that the low strike is still the funda-mental factor in the whole technique and philosophy of pitch-ing. It's the closest thing to the unhittable pitch there is."

Turner runs the legs off his pitchers and that is one of the reasons they are strong down the stretch when the other mound masters are tiring and losing their stuff. "A pitcher," Jim explains, "doesn't pitch with his arm alone but with his wind and with his legs. He must rear back and throw his stuff off his legs. That's why a lot of guys weaken in the late in-nings. It is in the last three innings of a game that a pitcher in top physical condition has the big edge. The more running he does the greater is his total of complete games and the big-ger his edge over the batter in the tight games."

Still another reason why the Yankee pitchers always finish strong is Turner's firm belief in keeping his starting stars out of the bullpen. Whereas in recent flag fights the Indians and Red Sox and in 1950 the Tigers used their aces both as starters and relievers, Turner kept his out of the bullpen. Between them in three seasons Raschi and Ed Lopat have been used in relief only seven times. Raschi started 103 games in the three years and relieved just three times. Lopat started 94 games and relieved just four times. The exception, of course, is Reynolds who is strong and willing and one of the great relief pitchers of the game when he isn't starting. "But we didn't use him too much in relief," Turner explained, "until both Joe Page and Tom Ferrick had left us."

There you have three great coaches who've served the Yankees well. Tommy Henrich, too, did a great job in 1951. But as he himself will tell you, there just wasn't room for four coaches. "I'm a guy who likes to be in the middle of things," Tommy said after he'd turned in his Yankee uniform for the last time. "There just wasn't enough work for me in the current Yankee scheme of things. I couldn't stand the comparative inactivity so I got out."

But Old Reliable played his part. It was he who helped develop young Mickey Mantle into a serviceable, even talented outfielder over the brief span of a single season. Remember that the youngster had never played the outfield before that dark spring day when Joe DiMaggio announced that 1951 would be his last time around. He had been a shortstop at Joplin the year before but he didn't have the look of a major league infielder to Stengel. But he had the speed to make a great center fielder once he learned the knack of going after a fly ball. He was such a great hitter and so blazing fast that Casey knew he would have to find a place for him in the Yankee lineup. So he put him in Henrich's charge and nobody ever worked harder than the two of them did under the scorching Arizona sun.

The long hours of practice paid off, too, for Mantle was the starting right fielder for the Yankees in the World Series. He'd been through a tough season of ups and downs. He'd been a superlative sensation in spring training with a .402 batting average and the mammoth home runs he knocked over fences from San Francisco all the way back to New York. He came to the Stadium under the searing pressure of the greatest build-up since Joe DiMaggio's debut. But when he arrived in 1936 Joe was a seasoned ball-player. He'd had four years of top minor league ball behind him and he was almost 22 years old. But Mantle was just a raw kid with only one season of organized ball behind him and he was just 19 years old.

Mantle flashed and sputtered and for one brief stretch he had to be sent to Kansas City to regain his confidence. He'd been striking out too much and his poise had all but deserted him. So he went to KC, found himself, and then came back to the Yanks in time to give them a lift down the stretch. All the time, though, he'd been coming along as a fielder. "Now," said Henrich, "he'd stopped throwing like an infielder. He was rearing back and getting his body into the throw and the ball was coming in strong and on the proper level. I tell you he amazed me the way he came along, all things considered.

"Will he be able to fill Joe's shoes? That's a tough one. I think a lot depends on his determination and his willingness to work and make the sacrifices. His natural tendency is to be a trifle lazy but he fights it and I think with the incentives he has and the chance to make the money he can he'll give it a big wrestle." But he could never have come close or be as near ready as he is without the teaching of Henrich. Old Reliable was still paying off even after they put his bat in the rack for keeps. It's a good guess, too, that Stengel and the Yankees will miss him now that he's left the Stadium for good.